# EDUCATION
## VOL. I

# EDUCATION

by

OSTAP E. ORYSHKEWYCH, Ph. D.

## VOL. I

## THE PHILOSOPHY

## OF

## EDUCATION

with Forefords by

LEONARD A. McDONOUGH

THIRD EDITION — ENLARGED

PHILOSOPHICAL LIBRARY
New York

© 1966, 1979, 1982 Philosophical Library

Library of Congress Catalog Card Number: 82-80781

ISBN 8022-1246-8

Printed in the United States of America

*To his Mother, one of the finest authorities on the philosophy of life, the author dedicates this work.*

# FOREWORD

The *Philosophy of Education* is the title given to the first volume of a seven volume work under the general title — *Education.* In order to acquaint the reader with the need and value of this educational work I shall quote an excerpt from a personal letter addressed to the author by a distinguished professor from a prominent University in Ohio.

". . . with a penetrating eye, you have analyzed ideals that you believe should be involved in elementary and secondary schools. Likewise, you have dealt with learners, professional teachers, parents and other adults, state and local government bodies, social forces, etc., as each of them relate and interrelate, directly or indirectly to education. You have done this with a critical eye to society on both sides of the Atlantic Ocean."

After reading this profoundly intellectual work on general education, there may be some who will not fully agree with the author's reasoning and deductions, due perhaps to the fact that his views are original and are scarcely to be found in pedagogical works published in this country to date. Nevertheless these views and ideas are intensively apprehensive and thought-provoking, and should arouse due interest in an educator to further pursue their analysis and logic even though they may seem to conflict or collide with our present methods of education.

In conclusion, I wish to emphasize again the thorough and comprehensive research that went into the preparation of this classical presentation of new vistas in our educational system. For this the author deserves our gratitude.

*Leonard A. McDonough*

# FOREWORD
## *to*
## THIRD EDITION

In order to acquaint the reader with the value of this educational work I shall quote the review of this book made for the Clearing House by Dr. S.A. Moorhead, Dean, School of Education, University of Mississippi, University, Miss. in September 1967.

"In this essay Dr. Oryshkewych decries the dehumanizing forces impinging upon man in this modern day and looks for a renewed, revitalized education with a personal thrust as the best corrective for the problem. Man is dangerously threatened by a poverty of spirit, and about to be overwhelmed by the soulless technology which he has created. His spiritual impoverishment is reflected in an asserted deterioration of morals and aesthetics, and latter particularly evident in modern art and music.

The author's prescription represents an excellent example of a genre of philosophic idealism. Reference to such concepts as self-realization, a child's psyche, the primacy of reason, the natural law, the psychology of the will, the absolute idea, the ideal of personality, innate differences of mind and temperament, the necessity of spiritual resources, and the "drawing-out" of the child illustrate classic facets of the idealist position. This work might find its greatest usefulness as a type-study in comparative educational philosophy.

Dr. Oryshkewych writes with an air of continental detachment in a didactic, oratory manner, expressing himself more often in generalizations than in concrete terms and situations, especially those such as would be familiar to American teachers. His assumption of the necessary central authority of a state department of education in matters of curricular objectives, his opinion that the child has a right to choose his school but not his subjects, his apparent lack of sympathy with the "comprehensive" high school (as well as the newer European gymnasia) are examples of opinions not likely to find wide acceptability among American educators.

The book is clearly written and systematically organized. The reader does not need philosophic sophistication to understand this work, which has been designedly written without technical detail in order that it might be readily comprehended."

In addition, these views and ideas are intensively apprehensive, therefore aroused interest in an educator to further pursue their analysis. For this the author deserves again our gratitude.

*Leonard A. McDonough*

CONTENTS

*FOREWORD* ........................................ vii
*FOREWORD TO THIRD EDITION* ................. ix
*PREFACE* ......................................... xv
*INTRODUCTION* ................................... xvii
PHILOSOPHY AS THE FOUNDATION OF EDUCATION  1

*The Task of Philosophy* ......................... 3

THE PHILOSOPHY OF MODERN EDUCATION ...... 4

*The Need for Philosophy* ........................ 4
*Education is the Spiritual, Intellectual,*
*and Physical Growth of the Child* ............. 5
*Subject and Method* ............................ 6
*The Principles of the Method* ................... 7

EDUCATION AS SUCH ........................... 8

*The Spiritual Growth of Individuals* ............. 9
*Education as a Conscious Progress* .............. 9
*The Term — Education* ......................... 11
*How to Live?* ................................. 12
*What Separates the Old and the New School?* ...... 13
*The Goal of the Progress of a Person* ............ 15

THE PURPOSE OF EDUCATION ................. 16

*Order in One's Own Life — A Purpose of Education* .. 17
*Democratization is the Goal of Education* ......... 17
*Education is Preparation for a Full Life* ........... 18

The Philosophy of Life ......................... 20
The Culminating Point in an Educational
    System is Ethics .............................. 22
The Characteristics of an Ideally Educated Person .. 23

THE COURSE OF EDUCATION ................... 25

Educational Material ........................... 27

TEACHING AS A PROFESSION ................... 29

The Calling as Such ........................... 29
Pedagogical Intuition .......................... 31
The Intelligence of a Teacher ................... 31
The Main Tasks of a Teacher ................... 32
The Responsibility of the Pedagogue ............. 33
For a Deeper Limit in Teaching and Education ...... 36
Corporal Punishment ......................... 39
The Health of the Teacher ..................... 41
Knowledge of the Physical Nature of the Students .... 42
Our Idea of an Educator ...................... 43

THE SOCIAL HERITAGE IN EDUCATION ......... 44

Historical Sketch ..........................:.... 44
Communal Environment and Education ........... 45
The Environment and Education ................ 45
Tradition as the Basis of Education .............. 48
The Cause of the Loss of Character .............. 49

THE ROLE OF THE WILL IN THE

EDUCATIONAL PROCESS ................... 53

The Psychology of the Will ..................... 53
Definition of the Will ......................... 54
Our Unused Talents ........................... 57
The Power of the Will in Education .............. 59

*Work as the Chief Means of Forming Will and Character*   63
*Overworking and Its Unhealthy Results* ............   66
*The Self-Development and Self-Education*
*of the Student* ................................   68
*The Interest of the Students* ....................   69

MORALS AS THE BASIS OF EDUCATION .........   73

*Morals at the Present Time* .....................   73
*The Sources of Morality* ........................   74
*Moral Education* ................................   75
*The Formation of Personality* ...................   82

IDEALISM IN EDUCATION ......................   90

*Education from the Idealistic Point of View* ........   90
*The Idea and Its Importance* ....................   91

ESTHETIC EDUCATION ..........................   94

*The First Steps in Esthetic Education* .............   95
*The School as the Basis of Esthetic Education* ......   97
*Theoretical and Practical Studies of Art* ..........   99
*The Task of an Educator* .......................   102

ETHICAL EDUCATION ..........................   103

*Educational Ethics* .............................   103
*The Chief Task of the School* ...................   106
*The Dignity of the Student* .....................   106

CIVIC AND SOCIAL EDUCATION .................   113

*The Historical Development of Society* ...........   113
*The Task of Civic and Social Education* ...........   115
*Education in Two Directions* ...................   118
*The Government in Society* .....................   120

The Scale of Living ........................... 122
The Law of Freedom ........................... 123
The School in a Democratic System of Government .. 124
The Social Conscience ......................... 128

EDUCATION FOR HEALTH AND PRODUCTIVITY .. 129

Amusement as a Means of Intellectual Development .. 130
The Causes which Influence the Health of the Child
  Positively and Negatively ...................... 131
Education for Productivity ..................... 133

THE METHOD OF INSTRUCTION AND EDUCATION 137

Principles of the Educational Method .............. 142
Factors in the Improvement of Educational Work .... 145
The Need for Theoretical Knowledge ............... 148

EXPERIENCE AS SUCH ........................... 150

The Nature of Experience ...................... 150
Experience in the Hours of Instruction ............ 153
The School as a Source of Experience ............ 164
Psychological Judgments on Experience ........... 167

AUTOMATION ................................... 170

BIBLIOGRAPHY ................................. 175

INDEX ......................................... 185

## PREFACE

While visiting schools in the Eastern and Western Hemispheres to get a better understanding of the educational systems of both and of the methods of presentation of educational material, I was able to observe greater or lesser shortcomings in every school. This prompted me to make a deeper study of the educational and training programs of the public and secondary schools of the older as well as of the modern educational systems.

A study of these programs and numerous conversations with teachers caused me to arrive at the firm conclusion that the present purpose of education is to train a professional in the shortest possible period, or rather, to produce an automaton. At the same time, modern education to a great extent neglects to educate persons of value or stature in the broadest sense of these terms. The following material provides some degree of illustration of the image of these persons.

The second shortcoming is that in training a person to be a narrow professional, the school system attempts to accomplish this by artificial and unnatural methods which delay the expected result of the work, and, what is most important, negatively reflect on the psyche of young people.

This book does not indicate precisely in which educational systems the negative effect is most easily observable, because no throwing of a bone of contention against any particular system is intended. However, it is my wish for this book to serve to some extent as a lighthouse directing ships on the right course, regardless of the flags under which these ships ply the oceans.

*The Philosophy of Education* is the title given to the first part of a seven-part work under the general title — *Education.* Each subsequent part, as a complete volume, also has its title stating its contents more precisely.

The basic educational subjects *The Philosophy of Education* (one volume), *The Principles of Education* (two volumes), and *The History of World Education* (two volumes), are located in the first five volumes of EDUCATION. The next two volumes are additional. The sub-title of the sixth volume is *The American Schools in the Past and Present,* and the sub-title of the seventh volume is *The Modern Method of Teaching Foreign Languages.*

This volume primarily takes into account elementary and secondary schools. In some sections, I occasionally touch upon some questions which can also be applied to adult education.

In writing this book, I envisioned a worthy person as being one who must be skillfully educated, according to plan, beginning with the first grade of Elementary School. I also present, herein, the most important educational principles which can be easily utilized by parents at home and teachers at school.

Upon the advice of the publishers, I have attempted to make this book as short as possible, at the same time, including all the important educational principles and the most suitable methods for their implementation. Therefore, this book contains the essence of education, for all unessential explanations and examples have been omitted due to lack of space.

Purely philosophical questions are approached simply in order to permit every reader to derive practical benefits from perusal of this book.

O.E.O.

## INTRODUCTION

The war ended in 1945. Shells ceased bursting, but tensions in world affairs remained exactly the same. The consciousness of such a joyless post-war state, therefore, instinctively impelled us to prepare for self-defense, which endeavor is exhausting us physically and psychically, the more so as facts show the basis for our apprehensions. This period of post-war, political uncertainty is sometimes considered a transitional period, but if we analyze carefully the history of humanity, we will see that, from the very beginning of his existence, man has been compelled by the force of circumstances to struggle against all the difficulties in his life's path. If he did not conquer them, he had to perish so as to relinquish his place to the better and the stronger.

Every lull which follows difficult times must not be understood as the end of all troubles, for it is only the time appointed for gathering strength to meet still greater obstacles which will certainly demand much greater efforts on our part.

The production of atomic power made great changes in the conditions which had previously normalized the method of human life and simultaneously introduced humanity into the sphere of great possibilities. However, these great changes are not bringing happiness to modern humanity, for they admit the supposition that there might also be found particular individuals who might have the audacity to use this power for the annihilation of even a great part of humanity. Because of this, we feel especially keenly, at present, the need of a new philosophy which could solve the most involved complications of the modern period through a straight-forward method.

Philosophy, as a science, is not only a means for improving conditions, it is also the cornerstone of every creative act. Presently, we especially need philosophers who will have the courage to guide the individual nations, to reveal the inadequacy of their actions, for it now seems senseless to each of us to expend energy and money to attain another planet in the universe while at the same time we produce frightful weapons to destroy humanity and all its acquisitions during the millennia on our own earth.

In analyzing the important political aspirations of the individual nations, we very often observe in them a lack of logic, a lack of those basic principles of philosophy, without which we cannot imagine a cultured or even a civilized man. Analyzing these facts further, we certainly will all come to the single conclusion that we live in times when man has mastered matter and has produced automation, but simultaneously has become an automaton himself.

Modern man is a soulless automaton. He is fascinated more-and-more by a materialistic utilitarianism; therefore, he has entrusted his whole being to the dust-filled factory and is not even making the slightest effort, at least, to glance through the factory window from time-to-time at those roads which lead a man to his true goal.

The spiritual impoverishment of modern man is the chief cause of his esthetic impoverishment, which we can best note in painting, sculpture, as well as in literature. Each of these fields relies upon worn-out patterns which do not reveal the soul of the author. On the contrary, their content and form convince us that the author did not take into account their quality but only their quantity. And, so with every day, mankind is plunging with greater impetus into the abyss, and we cannot hope for any brighter future, because it is always the product of succeeding generations; and they will be such as the system which has reared them. The work of education has always been a great responsibility, and now this responsibility is increasing immensely.

The old nations were permeated with a sense of statehood, consequently, they were not concerned with the individual but were primarily occupied with the needs of society as a whole. So, also, today we can assert that the goal of education is the creation of strong social relations to which individuals of different social classes must be led. Therefore, we must so live and so educate the youth that the life of every individual will bring greater or lesser profit to society, for only then will the objective of education be achieved.

Education in ancient times fostered old traditions while, at the same time, it guaranteed the spiritual growth of society and directed educational activity. The ideal of education includes some certain amount of knowledge and understanding which, in the first instance, brings profit to society. Considered from the background of the present era, however, education can be considered a social activity, the value of which we can measure not only by the demands of the present but, certainly, also, by those of the future. Analyzing the systems of education, we can very often observe that the school is isolated from life to such a degree that it not only has no influence upon it, but it even draws no profit from life. It is rather something in itself — and for itself. Such a school separated from living sources never brings life to a higher level, but merely follows life at a very slow pace. We are able to feel the connection with life, chiefly, when the methods of life are more complicated, when they become the more obvious and urgent needs of the nation.

If we take the position that the school must be brought closer to life, we do not deny that education must rest upon philosophy, ethics, art, history, and especially upon politics, but politics understood in a responsible way, i.e., that correspond to the needs of the present time. But to a still larger degree, the school must rest upon psychology, for only by knowing the psychical qualities of children and understanding clearly the problems which confront society can it produce an ideal of education out of those specific values which lie deep at the bottom of the soul of the young people.

To educate means to extract from a child those inner forces which slumber in him, and to direct them. The dominant system of modern philosophy is pragmatism, adapted by James to education, which aims to educate the alert individual from the viewpoint of practical life. Unfortunately, very often we meet with this opposing argument: Those fields which have direct application to life have no educational values, but those which have no application to life can possess these values in a high degree. Because of this, there rises before our eyes a clash in the educational ideal, which includes individual elements, as the development of the individual, and social elements, i.e., those which prepare him for the needs of society.

We can easily solve this problem if we establish in the beginning the method whereby the valuable qualities of a child can be brought to the surface and trained. Then we see that there is a certain internal connection between the two elements. It consists of the development of the individual and his adaptation to the needs of society. Dewey, the creator of an educational system, states that the child is the starting point, center, and aim. The ideal of education is the growth and development of the child, and in xx

this there is inherent the fact that from this ideal come methods of instruction and, therefore, all the disciplines of instruction must correspond to the development of children and be accessible to their understanding. We must not understand this in the sense that the school should set up a special, new program for every child in accordance with his physical and psychical characteristics, but there must not be a great gap between the school programs and the psychical orientation of the children.

The chief task of the school is to develop the individuality, properly. Individuality, however, is produced not only by the influence of the external world which by its activity blends the elements of the soul, but it is produced, also, by the activity of the mind. At the same time, we must criticize that trend of education which overloads children with a great quantity of knowledge without taking into consideration the fact that the children themselves cannot see how it will be of any benefit to them in the future. A mature individual, if he does anything, does it from greater or lesser necessity or from interest; the activity of children also must proceed from these rational reasons. Why compel children to do what is in opposition to their inner tendencies?

The goal of education lies in awakening the spiritual resources in a child with the aid of instructional processes and in developing the child into an active and useful citizen. When we speak of the building up of interest at the outset, we must remember that it should not come through compulsion, for if it does, it will not be maintained for long. If our teaching will be based on interesting the child, control and even the evaluation of subjects will be superfluous, for the child will be eager for the answer and will himself set to work. The child usually becomes introverted when he sees that the material to be learned is increasing daily and that it is not in his power to learn it. Then knowledge disgusts him, oppresses him, and this brings no profit either to his mind or his physical strength but merely undermines his health and leaves him with future bitter memories.

The most popular slogan of modern education constantly places foremost the demand for the independent development of the physical and spiritual powers of the pupil, for the time has already come when we must finish with study which is based only on the assignment and explanation of homework and its correction. We must turn our main attention to independent work in school in all scholarly subjects.

The pupil ordinarily must not be forced to assimilate vast amounts of scholarly material, but when he must do so; he must not work long outside of school.

As to the question of educational ethics, it must rest on the completely natural tendencies of the individual. By these natural tendencies, we must understand the corresponding series of psychical qualities which the educator can never destroy or increase but, at best, through his wise conduct can guide and perfect.

In the section of this work on esthetic education, there is pictured to some degree the spiritual impoverishment of modern man, which goes hand-in-hand with his esthetic impoverishment which we see primarily in artistic works. The fear of such impoverishment is the chief reason why the problem of esthetic education is of extraordinary importance at this time, for it embraces the dominant features of the pedagogical ideal. Esthetic education is also an important element of the development of the modern cultured person; it polishes him, makes him able to accept artistic, unattainable, intangible truths not connected with mathematical proofs. Esthetic education uplifts the desolated egos beaten down by the sorrows of the present day and places them on the road which leads to an harmonious union with the first cause, to union with the Creator of both the microcosm and the macrocosm.

A further mission of pedagogy and the philosophy of education is the training of the pupil in the spirit of the state and society. This task of the educational process must never be ignored. Education in the spirit of the state and society traces its roots to the past, to those times when the social spirit of all humanity was taking shape. So at this particular time, an era of coming new events in the world, it must be the task of the teacher to make the greatest possible efforts to furnish the greatest possibilities for the strengthening of the spiritual as well as the physical organism of his nation.

It must be the task of the educator to adapt his nation to the mission which it has to perform for the good of all humanity. In this connection, the state and society must first create a suitable atmosphere and physical conditions so that the school can develop its educational activity more advantageously for the youth and so that the youth can better advance in the educational process.

The school must also take care that the young develop in their souls a consciousness of citizenship, for the problem of social relations is nothing else than a problem of conscience. In no case can there be any question of the rebirth of a man if he has ceased to be conscientious. All programs, all statutes, and all laws come from the people and are in turn applicable to the people. So on the conscience of these people depends their content and method of application to life. A conscientious person is like a link in the actions of the whole of society. With the aid of his conscience, the individual must settle his own accounts with society, with which he is essentially united.

These then are the chief problems which will be discussed in more detail in the individual sections.

EDUCATION
VOL. I
THE PHILOSOPHY
OF
EDUCATION

## PHILOSOPHY AS THE FOUNDATION OF EDUCATION

The term philosophy can no longer be understood, today, as it was some twenty centuries ago. In our time, philosophy is a practical vehicle designed for mankind to make work and life easier and pleasanter under widely different circumstances. It is accepted generally that a strong link exists between philosophy and education which can be readily observed in the history of philosophy. The educational doctrines of such eminent philosophers as Plato, Spencer, and Locke were no more than the practical application of their philosophical views. Moreover, the philosophy of teaching and education possesses the special feature of being compelled to grow ceaselessly and remain in harmonious relationship with the instincts and feelings of the individual. The thinking of society never dare outgrow it. The purpose of education is to inspire in the young a true relationship with the problems of life and, at the same time, stress the tendencies along which the process of education should develop.

Philosophy is the core of all principles and worthy motives. It is the authority on which rests the trust of the young in their parents and teachers. It is, at the same time, the inspiration for our plans; the latter are systematized concepts and judgments. Consequently, philosophy is the basis and solution of all problems.

Philosophy is also the source of principles and arguments by means of which we are able to understand the goal of human life, being at the same time the foundation on which rests all forms of knowledge: art, literature, morals, religion, and all culture, including civilization. The extremely personal problems of our souls find lucid explanations, therein, as well.

Philosophy is a science which every person can use at almost any moment and stage of life. It embodies the achievements of the thinking of individuals. For well over twenty centuries, people of different social classes and classifications have added their achievements to those of their predecessors and have handed them down in a different form. Philosophy also finds a place in its range for facts from the field of physics, those of concepts and images. Its task is an unceasing search and examination of the physical world, the life of man as an individual and also of society. It unceasingly controls life and all existence and strives to view them as a whole. The merchant and the poet look at life differently. Philosophy wants to see life and existence as an observer of all periods and all existences would see it.

Philosophy is the basis of all science. It has separated us from the external world and it has created a corresponding rational world for our soul. In the most general sense of the word, the term philosophy, is the knowledge of things from their deepest causes, and philosophy attains this knowledge with the aid of the natural light of reason. Philosophical knowledge has three characteristic and fundamental attributes:

1. Fundamental
2. Comprehensive
3. Most unified

Possessed of these three fundamental characteristics, philosophy attempts to discover new knowledge in connection with *Truth, Beauty,* and *Good.* It defines their place in the sum total of reality.

Philosophy is separated from the experimental sciences not in essence but only in form and method. In addition, philosophers are never satisfied with those results which they receive directly through experience. They seek the prime causes in everything and classify every individual thing in its relationship to the principle which produces it and consider this as one element of the whole complex of the systems of knowledge. When it is a question of teaching and education, philosophy has the task of indicating the true path by which young people should reach into the depths of their lives.

Philosophy is, as it were, a body in which all principles are included on which not only must teachers rely during the educational process but also parents who wish to make their children capable of effective, practical life. The very essence of the word "philosophy" (friend of wisdom) includes teaching and education. Therefore, not only teaching but education must be based upon philosophy. It grows into the life of a person as deeply and broadly as it alone can, and it receives its form from the heart and mind of the person.

Because it is the summary of all branches of knowledge, philosophy automatically emphasizes directions, leads humanity, and dictates to men. It makes every effort to make the present agreeable to a person and the future even more agreeable. With this purpose, it dictates the modern principles of education. Meanwhile, it continues to grow, its growth, however, proceeding in harmony with man's instincts and feelings.

## The Task of Philosophy

At the present time, when the human mind is imbued with military techniques, when all energy and all efforts are turned toward the power of destruction, it is difficult for the ideas of philosophers to break through the clouds of atomic explosions, through the walls or armored weapons, through steel and concrete shelters, to enlighten a person with their radiance and show a proper direction for his actions. Modern, civilized man is often like a wild beast in the jungle which fully believes in its physical strength, for it owes to it many of its triumphs. But man forgets that there are moments in life in which powerful strength of itself can be the cause of his ruin if he relies upon it too much and so overvalues it. Thus, a nation, although physically strong, will more-and-more approach its destiny of disintegration if human reason, wrapped in emotions, does not take control of the power of modern, military techniques.

It was the desire of the philosopher, Plato, to see reality firmly and in its totality. In the range of the understanding of reality, man occupies one of the chief places. Therefore, the philosopher of the modern period must, in various ways, transfer his deep thinking to the field of the scientist. He must discover all knowledge and the best method of approach to the nature of reality. At this period, a period of industry, when technique has usurped all the powers of a man, philosophy must show a man his real ideals and convince him to serve them. The machine is nothing but a tool with which a man has the right to profit. However, the machine cannot be a passion which darkens the reason of man to such an extent that he reveres the machine and sacrifices himself to it. The machine is a great tool of man which must serve only for the good of humanity and never be a source of its destruction. Yet, at the same time, philosophy does not dare to permit contempt for the laws of nature. By nature we must understand not only physical nature of man, universally, but primarily we must ascribe to human nature the soul of man, thanks to which man is a rational animal.

## THE PHILOSOPHY OF MODERN EDUCATION

The philosophy of education differs from the art of education. Knowledge reveals new facts which not every one can perceive without adequate training. Philosophy, however, accurately defines the significance and importance of individual facts. It does not give us new facts. It only gives the answers to questions relating to fundamental causes as well as an accurate indication of the facts.

We develop knowledge with the aid of an appropriate method, i.e., a method of objective studies. Studies of this kind are verified by tests in each individual discipline. The philosophy of education attempts to unite the different functions and aspects of education, and has as its goal the indication of the importance of education which is the result of every properly arranged educational process.

*The Need for Philosophy*

Every individual has his own philosophy of life. One, an optimist, looks at life through rose colored glasses; another, a pessimist, constantly turns his attention to the dark side of life; still another generally will not bother about these problems. It is not important how a person thinks about life and how he estimates its values, for his own special mode of thinking is his philosophy. But the teacher of the philosophy of life immediately must show the path which leads into the depths of life through the classrooms and the halls of educational institutions. In pointing out the direction, he carefully must take account of the fact that the importance of the process of education is greater than that of all other processes. There is no other occupation in the world on which the fate of present and future generations of individual nations and of all mankind may depend. Hence, the activity of the teacher must be based upon a philosophy of life. He must love children and not dare to neglect their natural inclinations. For a teacher by profession to have his own philosophy of life, he must also study another philosophy: the philosophy of education.

Time, like water in a river, brings the new to replace the old. Thus, the methods of education and teaching forever lose their old forms and adopt the new.

It is a too generally accepted idea that education is nothing more than the preparation of young people for later life. Education is something more than preparation for later life — it is life! It is an uninterrupted process from the beginning to the end of life, whether in school or after it.

It is the task of the modern teacher to conduct himself with the student in such a way that the student feels that he is being treated as a reasonable person and that the problem on which he is working is important in life. If the teacher treats a child in this way, the child will live his own life from the first day when he crosses the threshold of a school to the last moment of his life.

*Education is the Spiritual, Intellectual, and Physical Growth of the Child*

Very important problems for the teacher are to consider whether the growth of the child has a truly healthful direction and, if necessary, to direct his way. The three-dimensional growth of a child, which really begins in school and continues as long as the person lives, is the chief aim of modern teaching and education.

Teaching is the uninterrupted enrichment of experience, for, as long as teaching continues, teachers are constantly adding new elements. At the moment when teachers add new experiences to the old, there automatically occurs a reorganization of all thoughts and actions of teachers, and they always take the new experience as a new basis. Progress is the essential aim of the philosophy of modern teaching and education.

The philosophy of Dewey considers it necessary to put a goal before the student before every separate step in teaching. At that moment, when the teacher places the goal before the student, spiritless and mechanical teaching is transformed into a highly valuable art which develops, enobles, and improves the whole life of the person from every point of view. Therefore, the attainment of goals in the learning process is the greatest factor in life.

Facts, as such, never have a stable significance in life if they are not repeated or if they have no steady relationship to newly appearing facts. The work of the teacher lies specifically in the search for new facts, basing the course of his actions on facts worked out and perfected by the new teaching method. The point of attraction in this case comes from the newly established facts and points to the needs of the pupils and society. This directing of the point of attraction in the educational process makes the relation of the teacher to his work an important factor in the teaching process.

The teacher, first of all, must make his own main effort constantly persevering. We have learned many subjects in school. We have understood many things sporadically which today we have almost forgotten and of which we have retained scarcely anything, but what is left is very important, i.e., the relation between these forgotten facts, or, in other words, a survey of the subject. The best sculptor to produce this point of view with the greatest delicacy is the teacher. For this reason, his work has fundamental significance for individuals as well as for society.

The teacher is not able to foresee all cases and possibilities with which the child will be confronted in the future, but he does have the means of defining the direction along which, if followed, the child will be able to guide himself in all instances on the pathway of his life. The teacher by his teaching is giving the child a survey of different subjects. He is giving the student taste and evaluation. All of this simultaneously is forming the character of the person.

*Subject and Method*

There are various views on the importance of subject and method. In the old school, the subject held first place. This partially can be justified when teachers take into consideration the fact that the pupil after finishing the elementary and intermediate schools is to continue further studies in higher schools, or, in another case, if we assert that knowledge is the subject and method of education. But, if, based on the pattern of modern teaching and education, there can be made a completely different statement that education and life are nothing but synonyms. If the process of learning and education is considered as a process of physical, spiritual, and intellectual growth, then the method is much more important than the subject. This should not be interpreted that in present day schools we are placing the subjects last, but we do emphasize that it is the problem of the school first of all to find a method that will permit the children both to live a pleasant life in school and to develop in the aforementioned three dimensions.

## The Principles of the Method

There are various views on the method. A narrow view describes the method as the indication of a specific direction to accomplish the work in the best way.

A second, broader opinion asserts that the method is not only a direction and that teachers by following it, accomplish some mission, but it also takes into account all the factors which are involved in accomplishing the mission. Depending upon the quality of the work, the teachers choose for it an appropriate method. The chief cause of faulty instruction is a narrow method. Sometimes, the teacher tells the children to read, and they read for hours, but they do not understand what they are reading. Consequently, a narrow method is in no way able to give a good result. The function of the educational method is, rather, to be the bridge which connects the child with knowledge and society. This marks the complete fulfillment of the educational journey.

The most important factors which indicate the principle of method are ideas which test the method, i.e.:

1. The goal of teaching and education,
2. The needs of the community,
3. The psychic and physical health of the children.

As for the first point, the nature of the subject and the trend of the action at the time of its realization is defintely noted by the teacher, and he again, in defining it, takes into account the goal which inspires realization.

The second point which determines the method of instruction and education relates to the needs of the community. This point, in turn, interrelates to the third point. If the community wishes its members to stand morally and intellectually on a proper level, it must interest itself in the education of its children in the schools and not merely care for their material well being.

## EDUCATION AS SUCH

Education, as such, at first glance, can be of no interest, attracts in no way to itself, but seems rather a dull routine. But in looking into it more deeply, we immediately become more amenable to the educational process because we see definitely that education places a person in his proper place in all situations. It implants in the soul of a person a special capacity which in all circumstances advises him how he can show his personality in a given situation. This capacity in a person shows his attitude toward his moral obligations, his concern for the truth, his concern for integrity toward others, and it teaches all the best forms of social conduct. If in this context we use the term personality, it is important to understand that we do not identify it with the other psychological term individuality. The concept of individuality is of narrower context than the meaning of personality.

Individuality denotes an organic wholeness. It also takes no account of the external world to the point where it even subdues all the actions of external factors and applies them to the demands of his own internal ego. Personality, however, has all the attributes of individuality, but, in additon, it has another quality: consciousness. A personality is aware of the fact that it is separated from the external world and that it is living its own life. This last quality is peculiar only to man, for only a man consciously places before himself definitely determined problems and compels all nature to serve his needs. But a person is born only with signs of consciousness and not with a full consciousness, for this gradually is developed in a person. In its formation, such factors often take part as temperament, talent, and surroundings; in the formation of personality, they develop character, and it tells most of the given personality.

Education is of great significance for its good result may often reach important proportions. A child receives all his important knowledge from his teacher not only by oral instruction but, primarily, from the example of his superior. The child grasps everything by uninterrupted observation, which is peculiar to a child, and this awakes in the child the desire to follow his educator. Furthermore, the personality of the child is enriched by the subjects studied in school: literature, history, and art, in the broad under-standing of the word. These acquisitions of the child are the real bases of his industrial, social, and even political activity of the future. Thus, education increases the spiritual values of the indi-vidual, and these will reveal his personality at every step and in that degree in which he possesses them.

Speaking of the culture of any people, we actually refer to these above-mentioned spiritual values which, depending upon their quantity, place the nation on a certain level or above it.

## The Spiritual Growth of Individuals

The spiritual growth of individuals is the development of human-ity in its full consciousness. The world adopts that form which humanity gives it. When we speak of the world, we understand primarily the physical and spiritual worlds. The second can be divided into many worlds, but the most apparent is the world of spiritual values where these are at the lowest level — the world of the streets of great cities. By this world, we generally understand it to be the city rabble which places its dexterity in robbery and brawling as the highest point of its perfection and life productivity. So this world does not owe much to schools, it is rather being educated by the organs of investigation, prison cells, and houses of correction for minors.

Opposed to this world is another world of people who have sin-cerely devoted their lives from childhood to work for progress and for the good of humanity. The unrestrained power which put them on the path of self-dedication and renunciation, which showed them the trend to scientific and artistic activity, is the definitely defined method of their education, and for this they are primarily indebted to the school.

## Education as a Conscious Progress

We can without longer reflection say that the world of the progress of the principles of the intellectual as well as physical development of education is conscious evolution. Its main task is to achieve the highest level of progress, raising the young of the present to the highest level of both spiritual and physical develop-ment. All educational institutions try to submit to this great ideal.

The main problems of the present time are not important in comparison with the problem of educating the youth of today, because all the evil tendencies and habits are an inherited disease, passing on to every new generation, and multiplying in the process. So, if in our free moments we ponder our future, when our youth today completely lacks all honorable traits, we can pose the question: Who in the future will be an honorable physician, judge, teacher? Can we assume that their work can be done by a man who does not have these virtues? Everything cannot be replaced by sports. Although sports dominate in the modern school, this does not mean that this is correct, that it is truly good. Old Rome also forgot the virtues and dedicated its entire life and existence exclusively to the demands of the body, which soon brought about its downfall.

All the great problems of the present day are nothing compared with education. The future of a nation depends fully upon the system of education of the constantly succeeding young generation. Among the great obstacles to education, must be included the fact that too many young people, yet in their early years, believe stubbornly in their own maturity and proficiency under all conditions, and, furthermore, scorn the advice of parents, teachers, and elders. It must be stated truthfully that the present day school not only tolerates this but even evades the problems of training, basing its views on the premise that the question of training does not lie within the field of its competence.

Such a concept of the aim of the school is completely erroneous, for the school is not an establishment where dogs or parrots are trained, it is an institution. On its activity depends the existence or non-existence, not only of individuals and the nations, but of all humanity. So as not to leave this charge unjustified, let us consider an example: If one entrusts the frightful inventions of modern technology into the hands of a person who does not have a mature mind or human feelings, what will be the results? Perhaps, at first sight, this charge may seem self-contradictory, for modern man has risen so highly intellectually that he has been able to make great unparalleled growth and progress in technical knowledge and in medicine, by which he deserves to be called not only a civilized but a highly intelligent person.

The achievements of modern technological science, are only achievements in one direction. But for a man to be considered intelligent, it is not enough to know mathematics, physics, or chemistry, for then the school would be like the naive builder who began to build a large house but erected only one wall to its full height and left all the other walls unstarted. The builder did this because it seemed to him that it was the most advantageous way or perhaps the most economical. That is also the impression given by the education of the young. We read in the newspapers and journals that we have lagged behind because of our lack of mathematicians and physicists. Let us, therefore, venture a question: How do we stand in the other disciplines, in literature, history, art, and others? It is exactly these disciplines which broaden man's outlook on all life's problems, make the ordinary person into an intelligent human being, endow man with certain graces, and make him noble. Now let us ask again: Have we perhaps surpassed other peoples in these disciplines? It is necessary to reiterate: If we think of ourselves as true builders and plan to erect a tall building, then let us build all four walls at the same time, for otherwise any gust of wind would blow it down, burying the naive builders under the ruins.

Education only then is defined accurately if the subject determining education proceeds from its main purpose.

Ethics very often employs a definition which appears perfectly adequate: Education is the realization of oneself on the highest plane. Its purpose also is to educate an individual to know how to live, enjoy life, and to serve society with a full measure of devotion. Each individual has his own strictly defined values in greater or lesser degree. These values can be very active or just barely able to act, but it is they which make the person valuable to all society.

### The Term — Education

In its broad sense, the term education describes activities containing all the influences to which a person is subjected. Education awakens all the talents of a person, directs his habits in the right direction, forms the character, and makes the individual into the person whom society subsequently comes to know.

Education also signifies the end result affecting the method of thinking of the individual and his sense of moral values. Education means the development of a person's spiritual as well as physical powers. All this adds up to make a person's life productive. It has been known since ancient times that the result of the activity of the student is as rich as has been his teaching and education in schools. But the quality of education depends not only on the capabilities of the teacher but also in large part on his experience. Experience, next to inborn talent, is the major factor which places an individual on one level or another.

*How to Live?*

How should one live not only in the material sense of the word but in its broader connotation? There is an answer to this question: To live properly and live well means to guide one's activity so that it is correct in all aspects and under different circumstances. This not only refers to the great actions of a person but to his everyday deeds as .well.

Such a definition is very broad, but it is impossible to give an answer to all questions concerning a mode of life, for the life of every individual is very diverse, the more so as his circumstances are constantly changing. But every school steels the character and inspires in the child a skillful approach to people and a most reasonably developed method of thinking so that, taking it all together, it renders him capable of living with his fellow men under all conditions. It makes a person able to perform masterly and magnanimously all his tasks, both private and public, in times of peace and war.

The school must develop first in the child a strong will which would compel the body to obey his commands, and not vice versa. Hence, the education of a child must be based on principles of reason. Plato (The Laws) says that a good education ennobles the body and soul and gives them the greatest perfection and beauty. Education can be defined more broadly as the process of multiqualitative means, the task of which is to make all the actions of people more useful for themselves and society. The life of a person cannot be limited only to the assimilation of the achievements of his ancestors, for then mankind would never progress, but will stand merely at dead center. It is the task of the school to train the young so that they do not ignore the old achievements but, at the same time so that they feel the need for going ahead, thus perfecting their own personal life and that of society.

In analyzing the values of learning and education, we can compare them to a blazing torch which casts its light into the greatest darkness; they foster the talents of genius and, in ordinary people, they arouse creative capabilities. These two streams, learning and education, have come to us from hidden sources in the past already forgotten by men; they have come to us through long centuries along a hard road — thus having acquired laurel wreaths. They move ahead unceasingly, not considering great obstacles, and so have come to our days. Their basic object is to make us happy and, further, to transmit our happiness to those who come after us, so that they too can achieve our happiness and perfect it still more. Learning and education never stand in one place; they move forward, for by their very nature they are progress. They are the creators of culture and, at the same time, a form of fate. Philosophy, knowledge, and art are the works of their hands, and the school is the factory in which they fashion character. In it, they give certain direction to ideals, for they are the source of inspiration and a means to the goal of all desires.

## What Separates the Old and the New School?

The old method of instruction had only one task — to teach, and the task of the student was only to study and retain what was studied for as long as possible. First of all, languages including Roman and Greek literature were taught. The new school turned the attention of the teacher in a totally opposite direction. In the old school, the teacher turned his attention first to the subject of instruction, and secondly to the pupil. In the new school, the pupil occupies the first place, and the whole attention of the teacher must be concentrated on him. So the result of the present method is not determined by how much the pupils know, but by what they can accomplish themselves and how they regard themselves. Now, educators recognize that pupils are well schooled if they not only have knowledge of a given subject but if, at the same time, they can contribute something new, and, chiefly, can conduct themselves in life in such a manner that every one can recognize their schooling without difficulty.

The nature of instruction and education in the new school is indicated by the nature of reason, for we are able to develop and perfect only what we possess in ourselves. The schooling which includes instruction and education is nothing else but the influence of the teacher on the pupil, so that by this means the pupil would be able to achieve, exclusively by his own resources, everything in life. The nature of schooling generally is to give the pupil the courage required to implement his ideas into reality.

The idea of schooling is comprehensive. More accurately, schooling is the forming of the life of the student in accordance with natural laws, with national traditions, with the laws of religion, and with the conditions of personal and social life. It is the task of the school to make the pupil able to live in harmony with these laws and to limit the freedom of his own will in accordance with them. In the narrower sense of the word, schooling means the influence of the teacher on the pupil, with the aim of indicating the development of a suitably intelligent means of life which in the future will make it easier for the pupil to achieve the goals set by him. At the same time, present schooling is making great efforts to balance two elements, the personal rights of the individual and his obligations to society.

Schooling includes a well-thought-out plan of social progress. There is no other institution which can serve the state and the people as devotedly as the school. It is a power which brings society to order and also increases the might of the people. The school is the collection of all those ideas which society cannot neglect but must consider as something essential on which the progress of humanity depends. Education, as prominent pedagogues conceive it, is the highest and the most significant element of progress — the power of society. Furthermore, where there is no proper education, criminal acts are multiplied, the life of a man is shortened, the reasonable development of a nation stops, and the condition of its material life sinks.

The quality of the education of a given people can be recognized by its leadership and, also, by the devotion of society to work and solidarity. Education is the constant equalizing of pure desires with definitely defined advantages.

Thus, social progress is the result of the effect of different factors, or main influences, from which a person cannot be disassociated in any way, and very often it must become a factor of social improvement in whatever field it may be. The growth of mankind in the direction of freedom is progress which owes a debt primarily to the school. Progress is one of the most fundamental concepts of education. It has as its task the teaching and the educating of coming generations so that the people may steadily become stronger and, with every day, become more stable and productive. At the same time, progress is the ability to understand nature in the broader sense of the word, and it is the cultivation of ideals, tendencies, and views. Therefore, it plays a great role even in the daily activity of a person.

## The Goal of the Progress of a Person

The goal, of the progress of a person, is full domination, full control over all the circumstances of existence. There is true progress when a person develops physically and psychically and when this development is in harmony with the laws of human nature. At the same time, a person achieves good results from his physical activity, because progress which follows natural laws is able to utilize these laws for the beneficial and harmonious development of mankind. This progress also produces harmony in all relations of a human being, since it controls all human acts and inclinations. In other words, the importance of progress lies in the fact that it increases human knowledge and strengthens the will, and by this means a person is able to test his physical and psychic nature and keep all inherited or acquired inclinations under control.

## THE PURPOSE OF EDUCATION

For more than two thousand years, great educators and teachers have been forming the objective data of education into a system. Many devised their own educational systems which subsequently developed into their educational schools, practicing one method or another.

A careful analysis of all these theories and systems will lead us to the conclusion that they are in agreement on main issues, with differences appearing only in non-essential matters. The objective worth of all these theories lies in the fact that they are all aimed at a solution of the problems of essential values. An analysis of their works shows that the following are the problems with which they are most concerned and to which they devoted much time and many pages in their works:

1. *The problem of health:* How to preserve health; and, if poor, remedies offered for its improvement.
2. *The problem of relaxation:* When should periods of rest be taken, of what duration should they be, and what is the nature of true relaxation.
3. *Economic problem:* How to manage money so that it would bring financial independence and not lead into the great abyss of debt.
4. *The problem of family life:* What is true family life, and who carries the responsibility of the family.
5. *The place of the individual in society:* What is the rule of conduct for an individual in society and what is the relation of the individual to the state.
6. *The problem of progress:* What are the elements of human progress. Here the term progress was understood by the educators to mean intellectual and spiritual development, and not a race after material goods. The former was considered essential and the latter unimportant, and sometimes even harmful.

Focusing attention on the problem of educating modern youth, one comes to the conclusion that we cannot, under any circumstances, ignore the educational methods of ancient educators. This would be a great mistake. Instead, one must so adapt the old methods to the needs of modern practice that we would maintain a link with the past, but at the same time we must not allow any faulty explanation of the old methods or their misapplication in practice to make us the object of ridicule, or to halt the progress of education.

## Order in One's Own Life — A Purpose of Education

The next problem is a biological approach to the problem of putting our lives in good order. In the process of introducing this order, education is not only a motive power but an indispensable factor. By his very nature, every person makes an attempt to organize all the elements which make him distinct from the animal world, and, hence, place him on the highest level of living creatures. We call these elements strictly human, because they are associated closely with the demands of human nature; we place them on one side of the ledger. On the other side, we place maturity, discipline, and even the method of thinking of a person. We can call the first set objectives, since they are found to be present in greater or lesser degree in all humans; and the second set subjectives or formals, i.e., appropriate to individuals who have gone through a longer or shorter period of education. The two classes of elements are correlative, supplementing each other, and we must of necessity take them into consideration when we form a definition of teaching and education. At the same time, the connecting of these two elements and the proper subordination of them for the good of society and the individual is the chief problem of the modern — in the full sense of the word — teaching and education.

## Democratization is the Goal of Education

The modern system of education has the following fundamental task:

1.  To educate the individual into a fully valuable person and member of society,

2. To train the individual to be a productive worker,
3. To make a person able (suitably, reasonably, and healthily)
   to make use of his time at work and at rest so as to give
   him the power to continue developing his personality to
   the fullest extent.

When one thinks of true democracy, every individual, whether
he is an employer or employee, must have equal value and
independence. So, these three fundamental tasks of the educational activity must go together and never separate in the laboratory
of a democratic state, and no one phase of the three can be
neglected without peril.

The goal of education usually is established and directed to
the needs of the individual as well as to the needs of society. The
social order strives to educate the individual so that he can take
part in all the affairs of given groups with reasonable profit.
Whatever be the system of state order, in each of them education
will be dependent on the wishes and political tendencies of the
leadership. Under each political leadership, education must proceed
in accordance with the instructions drawn up by the chief leadership. But there is a question of something else: that these orders
must include democratic principles which, to a certain degree,
must have a place in every system of state structure. This healthy
understanding by the government of the importance of democratic
principles in the field of education will give the students a desire
for deeper studies for they will be convinced that their thoughts
and words will not be beating against a solid wall but will bring
them rewards in various forms.

### Education is Preparation for a Full Life

To live a full life means to devote oneself to everything in the
highest possible degree and to be happy at work and at rest. For
us to succeed in educating a person with such qualities, the
teachers must begin to educate him in this spirit from the
first classes of the elementary school. First, they must instill in
children a proper method of thinking. And, in this, the subjects
taught will be of great help. For through our teaching, we give
the child the possibility to train all his powers — not only his
reasoning, but also his moral, esthetic, and constructive powers,

and this must be done by intelligent and systematic explanations and discipline. The main aims are to discover and to develop in every pupil his dominating interest, within the limits of possibility of harmonious development, together with the general goal of education. In producing in the child an interest in continuous studies, the teachers must motivate this by explaining the fact that culture does not stand still but is dynamic; we move with it, or we are destroyed. By this method of teaching children we will provide them with a full education for a full life.

The teacher must take into consideration that one discipline interests a child the most, and the others somewhat less, but even if a given discipline interests a child the least, he must not ignore it and must try to master it, to some extent. Thus, the child will be developed on all sides of his nature. In a given case, one must limit the program by exactly defined boundaries and demands. The teachers must always take into account the desire of the majority of the pupils for any given subject. The subject which is most interesting to the students must be considered as dominant in a given school and, therefore, it must be placed on the highest plane, but the teachers cannot neglect other subjects.

The task of education must be to make full use of the natural longings which are aroused in young people and to guide them for the good of society. The pedagogue is first of all bound to recognize the aspirations in every individual child and in accordance with his individual psyche direct him to the above-mentioned goal. If teachers pay no attention to these aspirations or directly contradict them, they will thus prepare the soil for anarchy. Work which is done fondly ceases to be labor. It becomes even a pleasure. When it is removed from personal inclinations, it becomes drudgery, and its productivity lessens. So the very content of the life of a person depends upon whether the person is constantly creating something: new ideas, new values. It is the task of the school to help children in their creative work, and, if it does not try to develop these human values, it injures not only the individual but also society.

As we see at every step, the question of practical activity lies at a dead point in some schools. By this, they primarily harm the life of every individual who is so greatly dependent upon this practical activity. Furthermore, theory must be studied by the most capable students, for it is difficult, and not every one has suitable capabilities for theoretical studies. We have very often had occasion to see people with undeveloped intellectual capacities who should have completed technical schools. Instead, they completed gymnasium or college work, but by not mastering the theories sufficiently, they were incapable of further university studies.

This irrational craving for the higher schools, this great ignoring of trade schools in some states lead to the result that society cannot move forward, for its creative aspirations in the field of technical knowledge and industry will disappear. The school not only must not remain behind life, but it must raise the level of life and must accept the already established forms of physical and technical labor and perfect them, so that the young, when they leave school and go out into the world and life, can draw profit from them and bring profit to the community.

## The Philosophy of Life

The school first of all must acquaint the pupil with the true reality of life. This acquaintance, as it were, portrays before each of them an ideal toward which each pupil must aim, regardless of obstacles.

The acquaintance of the pupils with life means that the teacher teaches the pupil how to understand life in its various aspects and how to approach it so that life may not rebuff the child too early and the child be discouraged by his first failure, but rather follow a proper road and not the wanderings of prodigal sons.

Life is merciless and cruel, but a person can live well and be content with it if he knows how to approach it under all circumstances, knows how to conduct himself properly, and has an inborn or, at least to some degree, an acquired philosophy of life. The schools must teach the child this conduct without which he cannot take a step in life but will fall down and life will discard him as a dry, useless leaf until it casts him into the abyss for destruction.

Instruction in conduct must first rest upon the information gained from the teacher. The teacher must at every opportunity and by example teach the pupils how to conduct themselves in any circumstances. We must teach a child to be a philosopher in every situation. In our early childhood we already felt the need for a philosophy of life, and we searched for it. Today, however, we have forgotten this, and it seems to us that a philosophy of life is a subject of interest to older people and not to children. But this view is false, for a philosophy of life has its beginning in a child when he merely begins to be interested in various, even most trivial events in nature, as he begins to look for their causes. We have forgotten how many questions on the philosophy of life were answered by our mothers and how many by the teachers in school. We took this philosophy of life from many other sources, but these were childhood years, years of beauty and charm. Those years pass, and are followed by the fifteenth and sixteenth years of life and by the further years of striving for full maturity. These represent a great physical struggle. This struggle has its physiological basis in the sexual maturing of the adolescent and through the nerves it attacks the brain; he cannot always succeed in giving satisfactory arguments to keep on a proper moral level and not follow the passions of his lower nature. Here, there is need of a wise and authoritative teacher who, by his wise arguments and by his honorable and moral life, can convince the pupils that this is a transitional age, that after these years reason will triumph, and that a person must remain a person, for he has a much higher objective than merely satisfying his bodily passions.

The philosophy of learning and education demands the introductional classes which should be conducted by an older teacher for students approaching maturity. Such occasional lectures would always profit everyone, for they are a kind of armor which would protect a young student in this unbalanced, transitional period.

We have behind us many centuries in which civilization developed and culture flourished. There have been different systems of education, and each of them have tried to place their definite ideal before the students, their definite goal to which they were directing all their efforts. Each system had its own roads, its methods, which it considered best and put into practice. The chief ideal, to which not only the present teachers should direct education but also to which the teachers of many centuries subscribed, is culture in general, which consists of productivity, discipline, knowledge, the development of reason, character, spiritual and physical development.

*Culture* is the capacity to experience intellectual and esthetic pleasures; each person strives to possess it, for culture raises a person to a higher level.

*Productivity* is the capacity to accomplish tasks quickly and correctly. It is a necessary component part of every system of general education, for it is the source of progress of a people.

*Discipline* is, as it were, a sharpening of the tools of consciousness. It is that which prepares children for a proper future life.

*Knowledge* is the content of consciousness, determined by facts. In the preservation of the old and the creation of the new, knowledge will always be an integral part of a substantial education ideal.

*Character* is the controlling of a personal will.

The organization of the educational ideal, as one of the elements of the problem of education, lies in the realm of educational theory. In the matter of the education of properly good individuals, education must be directed toward culture, knowledge, and development; and if we also consider the welfare of the state, we must not neglect education in the fields of productivity, character, and citizenship. By an analysis of these given terms, one comes to the final conclusion that we are not free to neglect any of them in the educational system if we wish to have valuable individuals and a moral, healthy society.

### The Culminating Point in an Educational System is Ethics

The method or even the direction of education can be called experience, but at the same time the highest or final aim of education is ethics.

The aim of education is defined as experience, because it has still further tasks: it must arrange all experience and achievements in such a manner that their final systematization may have a correct relation to its highest and final aim. All these achievements, properly systematized, have that operating power by which the individual who follows their guide is transformed into a sterling person who lives a valuable and happy life, and every step of such a person, in a large degree, also helps others to make their lives happy. So, the final objective of their education can be called ethics.

The true perfection of all education is the full realization of the ideal of personality. In no case can the teachers denote the character of this ideal as physical, biological, or psychological features, but they must search for the highest quality terms which would denote accurately the importance of education and would also take into consideration moral and spiritual criteria.

The equipoise of spirituality in individuals is the ideal result of education. We must so educate that the whole body will obey the orders of the will based on the innate or acquired intelligence of the individual.

A good education always takes into account the inborn and acquired emotions in a person and does not try to destroy them but makes every effort to place these emotions under the full control of the reason of the individual and the opinions of society.

The principal goal of a good education is the perfection of a person. The teacher must always show himself a thoroughly upright person who, at the same time, tries to implant all his qualities in the child just as a painter wishes to make clear on canvas the image imagined by him.

Demonstration is one of the chief divisions of education. It also subordinates other auxiliary tasks: to increase knowledge in the child, to fashion a means of the clearest possible thinking, to strengthen discipline, and to create love for beauty and harmony and, thus, make the child a person fit for life and able to cooperate harmoniously with others. A good education has to foresee all the needs and demands with which life will confront the child in the future. It is impossible to prepare the pupil to face every special demand, but the teachers must rely first of all upon the natural educational process and also avoid hardening and scholasticism. So educate that the pupils know how to judge themselves and understand the value of the sublime ideals for which the school is training them. Life in the eyes of the children must be a valuable life, for otherwise the labor of the school goes for nothing.

### The Characteristics of an Ideally Educated Person

Looking at a well-educated person, we at once can almost with accuracy determine his intelligence and the system which educated him. The very posture of his body accurately shows it. A well-educated person always compels his body to obey the orders of his will, and best to observe this at moments when it is necessary to serve someone, to lift, or to offer something. It is exactly at these moments that we can easily notice the internal struggle in a poorly-educated person. In this case, reason commands him to serve someone, but the undisciplined body is like an unhewn log, and does not wish to obey the will.

The well-educated person always feels the need for going with the spirit of the times, always wishes to perfect himself further, whether by literature or by suitable companionship, or by high-quality theatre. The life of such a person is constant labor in achieving self-perfection. Such a person always takes part in social life, for he realizes that he is part of the community and profits by its achievements. Therefore, he has a special obligation to make some contribution for the good of the whole. He considers others — sometimes to such an extent that he seems superficial, and it even may seem that unlimited concessions are injuring him. He also remembers old friends and at the same time makes new ones.

Complaisance is a very important quality of a well-educated person, for he who thoughtlessly expresses his unjustified or even justified spiritual hurts cannot be called well educated.

The art of a good education lies in the fact that a person should know how to control himself, should not express his sorrow but should keep on working conscientiously and only his deeds should justify him, for they will justify him much better, since their justification is obvious and lasting.

A well-educated person always tolerates the thoughts of others, although they may be repugnant to him. Such a person always has a good will to help others. In all cases, he hides his disturbed nerves and tries to settle all matters, even the most drastic, as calmly as possible. He considers his family, cares about its honor, and never will bring his family affairs into the public forum. He loves nature, tries to understand it properly, and to have a proper approach to it. He rests all his judgments upon accurate data and not on assumptions. He makes all efforts to render his life much happier; he does not attach great importance to material things but ranks the values of the mind and spirit higher.

In a well-educated person at every step, there is always an exemplary order, for this order also exists in his soul. He will stand on the side of truth without considering that this may be to his disadvantage. He never scorns primitive work if he thinks that by any work he will improve his own life or the life of others. A well-educated man also knows how to pass his relaxation time in the best way. These are the general features by which we can recognize who is educated and the method used.

## THE COURSE OF EDUCATION

The chief tasks of education are to polish properly the character of each individual and to contribute to the development of his reason and morals. But to achieve this, one must first suitably organize the school which is to fit all the demands of the reasonable, moral, and physical development of the young of different ages. Here, the teachers must turn their attention to the need of a deep analysis of the subjects in the program of instruction so that they would not be stereotyped by dry routines but would correspond to the demands of the young of all strata. At the same time, they must comply with the method of education, the trend of which has been outlined by the leadership of the state. In general, the trends of education must be based upon:

1. Fostering the development of all moral as well as physical values of the individual,
2. A better and more correct understanding of the rights of nature,
3. Fostering the development of a better understanding of the demands and needs of society. The chief problem on which rest all the other problems of life is proper behavior in varied circumstances.

The problem of education also includes these questions:

1. How to develop intellectual capacities,
2. How to develop the body,
3. How to raise family life to a proper moral level,
4. How to produce good citizens,
5. How to improve all the sources which make a person happy to some degree and how to use all possible means to be not only one's self happy, but so that all may feel well in our presence.

These are basic questions — they are all serious, even though the form of life is undergoing various changes. To prepare a young person for a full life is the most important task of the school. It must classify first all these important questions and

place them in the order of their importance in the program of
instruction and education in the school. Their order would appear
approximately thus:

1.  In the first place we must place an educational activity
    which would teach a child self-preservation, to protect him-
    self and to be prepared for all situations.
2.  The child must be accustomed to perform fully the orders
    of his teachers and parents, and first of all he must under-
    stand the objective of these instructions.
3.  In all instructions which deal with each child separately,
    there must be some element which is concerned with the
    good of the community and state.
4.  Instructions must not ruin the joyful moments of young
    people, but at the same time these must be permeated with
    the spirit of true politeness.

In preparing a plan for educational work, one must first take
into consideration:

1.  The pupil
2.  The course of education
3.  The environment
4.  The teacher

We cannot reduce any of the four. The result of the educational
process always depends upon the harmony of these component
parts. The very concept of a course of instruction and education
includes not only the work of instruction and studies, but it also
includes all the occupations; all the school production; all the
exercises, activities and achievements. Here is reflected all the
motive power, all elements of the nervous system of every pupil.
The course must contain material which will apply during the
entire life of the pupil. The school must develop all the elements
of which the instructional and educational work is composed.
The object of educational activity is not concentrated exclusively
on furnishing the pupils a sufficient quantity of knowledge, but
chiefly on the ability to apply it practically in life.

When the teacher considers the elements of which the entire
educational process is composed, he must emphasize that their
value very often passes over into various stages of its situation.
The material the school uses, which comes from different times

and even different places, is based on the traditions and achievements of different peoples, which the school tries to improve upon and apply to the needs of both the social and individual life of the person. At the same time, the course must make clear the object of education. The object of education is a process resting on the broadest and deepest experience. The life of a person is a valuable life if it includes this process in all fields. The program of educational work in the school must be formed so that it constantly progresses, so that in the future instruction and education it will not need full reorganization. But it must work constantly, and this activity must be always in agreement with the spirit of the time and must be profitable as well.

The development of many-sided interests makes children willing to take part in all aspects of social life, makes them optimistic and valuable. The course of instruction and education in the educational system has approximately the same meaning as money in the economic life. The course of education and money are the tools of great social institutions, and as such they demand that they must not be forced from their proper positions but must be given the power to develop.

### Educational Material.

Educational material must be applied with great care to the psychic possibilities of the child. The school, before World War II, differentiated a person with physical and impulsive tendencies from a person with psychical tendencies, and such schools exist even today. In the psychical, the school made the greatest attempt to reveal a person with definite intellectual capacities, and here it made various subdivisions in diverse tendencies and tried to direct each tendency to appropriate disciplines, but in all this activity the school failed to emphasize sufficiently a consciousness of the goals and the feeling of the need to use them. Therefore, such education or such instruction cannot be called schooling or even spiritual progress. It is a waste, for it has before it a narrow range of activity in which it performs its task and does not try to develop other trends which are beyond its borders, which might assist in the intellectual and spiritual growth of the person.

"To educate" — says Dr. Georg Kerschensteiner — "means the same as to spread cultural values, i.e., religious, scholarly, artistic, moral, state and political ideas, and to make them the base of the coming generation."[1]

Elsewhere, John Dewey writes: *"A study is to be considered as a means of bringing the child to realize the social scene of action."*[2]

"But for our good thought to pass into a good deed of itself, we must be systematically trained to do this from youth."[3]

"All education must be commenced from the natural interests of students. The whole success lies in how far the educator will be able to join his intentions to the natural interests of the pupil."[4]

The future of nations depends on how the people succeed in replacing the blind obedience of subjects with establishing a feeling of obligation to turn an act into a doing.

There is a generally held theory that any trained disciplines influence the growth of others. Unfortunately, experience and practice show otherwise. Very often people quickly solve the most complicated mathematical problems; however, when on the same rules of logic they have to obtain a result in another field, as of politics, they solve it laboriously or cannot solve it at all. In the same way, the same holds true in the solution of life's problems. To solve the problems of life, each person must solve them throughout his entire life, from childhood, from the time when reason in greater or lesser degree begins to comprehend these problems.

That one discipline does not have influence in the development of another can be exemplified, at least, by the argument that one who has developed a good visual memory should also have a good memory for sounds. Yet, we see the opposite, for those who remember people's faces very often cannot remember their names. The most frequently demonstrated ability is that the perfecting of one psychic activity makes one able to use other qualities, even in diverse situations. This ability to apply quickly to various situations and to do the task as well as possible, according to psychologist Binet, is intelligence.

1. Kerschensteiner, Georg, *Die Pädagogik der Gegenwart in Selbst.* Bd. I, Leipzig, 1926.
2. Dewey, John, *Moral Principles in Education,* Boston, Houghton Mifflin Co., 1909, p. 31.
3. Kerschensteiner, Georg, *Ibid.*
4. *Ibid.*

## TEACHING AS A PROFESSION

It is that kind of a profession on which rests the responsibility for the young generation and the future of all humanity. All other professions are based upon the profession of teaching and education. The teacher, in the modern sense of the word, therefore, must be a teacher not only of a particular discipline or subject, but he must also be an educator. The authority of the teacher-educator cannot come only from the reason of his office, for his influence on the young will then be insignificant. The educator must have among other things all those qualities which are possessed by all the best leaders of groups, or nations. So, when we ponder on the person of a teacher as being a member of a profession, our ideas must always find their conception in this being a calling.

### The Calling as Such

The calling can be considered from various points of view but, for us, the important thing is that we consider it as first a psychic phenomenon.

To understand better the importance of a calling, we must distinguish between two classes of people: people who are born with a calling and people who have no special call. Considering these two kinds of people, we will see a marked difference from which it will be easy to discern the people who are born with the call.

In the current conversation, a calling is understood to be a gift with a definitely marked skill which may be greater or lesser. A calling can clearly appear in one or another skill or, in other words, through talent. Psychological classification divides a gift into general or special categories, where under the first it understands a certain level of intellectual capabilities of a person and tests him with the aid of various tests of giftedness.

Psychotechnology divides these tests into two groups: (1) synthetic; (2) analytic. The first have as their object to test in general the giftedness of a grown person or child, and the second tests the level of development of every individual intellectual ability as, for example, memory, comprehension, etc. This testing can be only a secondary means of investigating the talent of a person, for there can be other causes which can produce an incorrect result of the test. The more basic and more certain means is systematic observation and constant evaluations of the pupil over a considerable time. Actual giftedness lies in the inclinations of a person for a certain defined activity. It happens very often that at the time when capacity appears in children the parents pay no attention to it, and, in addition, there may be unfavorable conditions for its development so the capacity is ended with its first appearance.

Speaking of talents, (Who has them? How many does one have?) cannot be defined easily, for a person can have only one or can have five or more. Sometimes the person who has less ability can be considered as capable as the person who has five times more. To consider any one as talented, it is sufficient that his ability be greatly developed and only in one direction; however, if we consider a given person a genius, he must be characterized by a many-sided giftedness. He also must produce something new and original.

Besides the terms genius and talented person, there is a third term — a great person. We only call one a great person if he has had a broad but positive influence on humanity. Hence, such a great person is primarily one who had devoted his abilities to raising humanity to a higher level spiritually and materially. Very often capability is inherited, but it happens also that very talented parents produce untalented children.

Those people are really born with a calling who, at every step and in all situations, remain themselves.

To be one's self means the same as to be satisfied with one's self. So already we see here two categories of people: (1) Those indifferent to the effecting of this ideal and category; (2) Those for whom to be one's self is of a great value. Its accomplishment, therefore, is for them a question of life and death, for these talents with which they were born demand great exertions in order to manifest themselves even under very unfavorable conditions. At the same time, those individuals gifted with talents very often meet various obstacles on their path of life which must be overcome, so that the very effort to overcome the obstacles on the way to the realization of their thoughts is for them to be themselves.

Work in a calling is only a higher ideal-form, which holds **true** in every profession. When a person aspires to a profession, he at the same time feels and understands the art of the given profession. Every talent, as evidenced in the higher forms, urges the individual to self-revelation.

## Pedagogical Intuition

Pedagogical intuition appears in the individual uniqueness of a teacher. All creativity is a struggle, but pedagogical creativity is greater than any other. The pedagogical ideal is surrounded on all sides by enemies, and extraordinarily active vigilance must be maintained to protect it. First of all, the teacher must conquer those obstacles which arise from the individual nature of the children. He must not only aid the development of the previously noted nature of children but, frequently, he is even obliged to cross the nature of the child in order to achieve his ideal.

The material with which the pedagogue has to struggle is of various kinds. The teacher and educator must be no less active in connection with the teaching material if he wishes to be a living intermediary between it and the classroom of children. The teacher must be creative. He will be creative only if he himself will set aims for his own creative thoughts. In emphasizing the importance of intuition to a pedagogue, it must be asserted that intuition in a pedagogue does not in any way differ from the intuition of an artist. It discloses a foreign, spiritual world in its real entirety. It translates dead didactic formulae into the living language of images and feelings. It embodies all the trends and natural inclinations of the child in its pedagogical ideal.

## The Intelligence of a Teacher

Speaking of the indispensable qualities which a proper teacher must have, he must first have extremely high intelligence. This is the first of the marks of a properly qualified teacher. Knowledge and the use of good forms show that the calling of a teacher has fallen into the hands of a proper person. Intelligence gives the teacher a strong base on which he will rest not only the deep value of his calling but also the means of passing his hours of teaching, his approach to the children, and his common life with the teaching staff, but first of all it gives the teacher a real authority. An intelligent teacher has developed his so-called professional spirit to a high degree, thanks to which he has his own individual approach to the children and, hence, his lectures are valuable and optimistic. The teacher who is truly of good character is one in whom the forces that tend to good deeds always predominate.

Now, in analyzing bad teachers, i.e., those who have not chosen a proper profession for themselves in this case, they are divided into two categories: (1) Those who do not have a clear conception and thus their teaching is unclear and scarcely comprehensible; (2) Those who have a clear conception but cannot understand how the pupils are unable to assimilate so little of the knowledge which they, teachers, have arranged very clearly and accurately in their own heads. In analyzing the two categories of teachers, one can say that the first category represents those underdeveloped as teachers, and the second represents teachers who lack understanding. Both are included in the category of bad teachers, who are useless to any one. For the result of their work is usually very little, although the pupils often work very hard. Individuals with such little intellectual achievement or with an incomprehensible disposition must not strive to be teachers.

*The Main Tasks of a Teacher*

One of the first and main tasks of a teacher is to put his teaching hours on an appropriate level. The teacher must not only place his subject on the proper level, but, also, to a certain degree, must acquaint his pupils with other subjects that are directly connected with the main subject. In this way, the teacher teaches the children to form their own views on every question and not only to learn discipline; his teaching has a spirit and a deeper basis. During his exposition, he must use all secondary means, methods, and comparisons to enliven his teaching material and make it acceptable and easy for comprehension by the child. The more comparisons and repetitions in the given exposition, the easier to assimilate it. It is the further task of every teacher to develop at every opportunity all the powers and capabilities of the pupil. If he knows his subject properly, the nature of the child, as well as a philosophy of life, the teacher can boldly look squarely at his great task for he knows precisely what material to present in the process of instruction, how to organize his teaching, what approach to apply, how to carry on the repetition of old material, and how to support the new.

The wise conduct of the teaching hour, the organization of the teaching material, and its connection with auxiliary and secondary subjects is not a routine but a natural capacity which is united with the acquired intelligence of the teacher.

It is a further duty of every teacher to connect the teaching material with a philosophy of life. It would be a completely false mission of a school only to compel the children to learn the given material. The chief task which the school sets before itself is to teach the children a philosophy of life. All these subjects, in greater or lesser degree, are only a means by which the child more rapidly and with a certain plan develops his intellectual, spiritual, and physical capabilities. In this way, the child becomes daily more useful in life and constantly more versatile, for he has a completely correct approach to life and understands it better.

## The Responsibility of the Pedagogue

The pedagogue often is compared to a sculptor. Just as the sculptor takes a stone block and makes of it a statue, so the pedagogue creates from a child, like an uncut block, a definite finished personality corresponding to his own educational ideal. But there is one essential difference, for the sculptor is working with dead material, and the pedagogue is sculpturing beings who are living individualities with unique psychical and physical qualities. In connection with this, the responsibility of the pedagogue for the quality of his work is far higher than that of the sculptor. If a pedagogue by his approach maims the soul of a child, it will be not only a loss but, also, a crime against the child, his parents, and even society.

The activity of the pedagogue is the formation of a personality, and this the pedagogue must remember first of all. In this formation, his educational ideal must be the starting point as well as the concluding end. In large part, pedagogues upon going into a school often do not have their own ideal before their eyes, they often carry out their program of instruction in a mediocre way. Although a person by nature has his own individual peculiarities which must be developed in accordance with his nature, this does not mean that all the peculiarities of a child are good and that they all must be developed. A child at birth, besides his good inclinations, also has many inclinations that are not good, and these must be rooted out at all cost or directed toward a properly good goal. Bad inclinations are possessed not only by children of alcoholic parents or those sick with other inherited diseases, but, also, by children of parents who are considered fully healthy. Every child by nature has his own definitely marked psychological qualities, which are different in every child.

Theories of "free education" of such pedagogues as Jean Jacques Rousseau, Leo Tolstoy, and especially Ellen Key, can be now called utopias without the least hesitation. According to their teachings, a child itself must realize what cannot be done, because it will be to his disadvantage. They say that a child himself will come to the conclusion that in winter he must not sit at an open window if he is compelled, as a result of a cold, to stay in bed for a certain time. Such experiments, however, do not seem satisfactory to the parents for many reasons, for they bring with them non-advantageous consequences.

An opposite theory is the so-called theory of authoritarian education. The system of authoritarian education imposes the ideal from above, and the pedagogue is not obliged to pay attention to the natural inclinations of the child unless these inclinations affect the future occupation of the child. Yet, the pedagogical process is not only the development of the natural qualities, but a still more important element is the formation of personality. This forming of personality must not be brought about by means of violence but by a completely opposite means and in a humane way. The chief objective here in working out an educational ideal is not to put the pedagogue in the role of a tradesman and fulfiller of orders from above. Prof. H. Vashchenko solves the problem in the following way:

1. The educational ideal must be quite broad. It has to mark only the basic trends in the forming of the personality of the student. Such an ideal on the one hand gives the possibility of educating a child without doing violence to its nature, and on the other does not hinder the pedagogue in possibilities for creative work.

2. The educational ideal is worked out by the active participa-

tion of the greatest possible majority of the pedagogues as builders of the cultural life of their people. The form of this participation can be various pedagogical conferences, appearances at the organs of the state administration, participation in the press, and others. Such a means of fashioning a national educational ideal frees it from one-sidedness and guarantees the creative activity of the pedagogues.

3. Only those should enter pedagogical work who share the general trend of the educational policy of their nation. Those who, for example, do not share this should fight honorably and openly for their pedagogical views and should not introduce them secretly apart from the community idea.[1]

In these three rules, Prof. Vashchenko has summed up the task of a true teacher. In addition, everyone who wishes to work in the pedagogical field must be a psychologist. He must know psychology not only theoretically but, also, practically. The teacher must be able to know the individual child's soul and experiences, otherwise, he will adhere to trite slogans, and his teaching will bring neither satisfaction nor profit to the student. He will then be aware that he is merely an artisan.

The pedagogue must be extraordinarily perceptive, and here his innate intuition will help him. He must know how, at a given moment, a student is living, what he is thinking, and he must be able to recognize all this very easily by the changing expressions and reflexes of the student. The pedagogue must be by nature an artist, for this gives him another approach to his students and an influence on the forming of personalities. When pedagogical activity becomes only a trade, and this happens when the pedagogue looks on his work as a means of livelihood, then the work of this pedagogue loses its originally good creativity and; thereby, becomes uninteresting and even boring not only for the students but for himself. The pedagogue must not be an automaton. Coming to school, reading his lectures without putting himself into them, and merely repeating the same thing turns him into a mute and soulless machine. He becomes someone alien and indifferent to the students. Then the pupils have a general desire to be rid of

1. Vashchenko, Hryhoriy, *Vykhovannya Voli i Kharakteru,* London, Caplin and Co., Press Ltd. Croy don, 1952, Part I, p. 9.

him as soon as possible. In such an atmosphere, it is impossible
to think of pleasant and useful teaching and education.

## For a Deeper Limit in Teaching and Education

The future of a people is always reflective of its present generation, and it again will be such as it is educated to be. Therefore,
the goal of education is the knowledge of so guiding the life of
individuals that each of them will bring more or less profit to
society. The teacher must place before the eyes of the individual
the needs of the whole. Education, considered from the perspective
of the present day, can be regarded as a social activity, the value
of which we must measure not only by the needs of the present
but chiefly by those of the future. This goal of teaching and
education must not be either the over-intellectualizing of the school
youth or the overloading of them with a mass of knowledge, but
it should be the awakening, with the help of educational processes,
of their spiritual forces and the education of the young to be
active and valuable citizens.

To educate is the same thing as to spread cultural values and
to make them the cornerstones of coming generations. Our future
depends upon our success in replacing blind obedience with a
feeling of duty. Success depends, first, on how the educator can
connect his intentions with the natural tendencies of individuals.
The pedagogue must foster, first of all, the tendencies in every
individual child and in accordance with his psyche guide him to
the intended goal. If the pedagogues pay no attention to the natural
tendencies of the children or contradict them, they will warp the
young and prepare a basis for anarchy.

The teacher must consider the natural tendencies as the starting
point for further activity, organize them and, thus, from chaotic,
disordered efforts mold them to be conscious, independent, and
useful. The teacher must treat every student as an individual. It is
time to abandon the old and exhausted pattern of education
which was known to every old teacher, for it was not very hard
to learn. With this hoary pattern, which included in its content an
important amount of the elements of medieval instruction and
education, he tried to destroy the inner values in a child by fright-
ening him. He took away the freedom of thought, stopped the

development of the mind, and did this to achieve his goal at the least cost. The child, going to school, went as if to slaughter.

Much greater achievements in knowledge and education are secured by a completely different method, opposite to the preceding, one that is enlightened and delicate. By this method, the child sees in his teacher his own father, a friend to whom he will tell all that is in his heart, for he knows that the teacher is not holding a stick over him. This method must be introduced into the schools. Corporal punishments must never be practiced in schools. As positive proof that a bruise does not hurt on the body of another, there is cited the following example: This author knew a teacher who never went to teach without a stick in his hand, but when it happened that the teacher in another school beat his son, he did not hesitate, but at once hailed him into court. At the same time the teachers must here emphasize that they must not assume that the old method of education developed criminals and outlaws, but the main thing is that this method was bitter for the children as well as for the teacher who was truly intelligent. The content of the life of a person lies in the fact that a person is constantly producing something — new ideas, new values. It is the task of the school to aid children in producing these, and if it does not try to develop these human values, then it harms not only the individual but society as well.

To create good properly, one must first limit one's activity, one must find his own environment from which comes his thought and his attention, and one must solve not all but only some questions and work within these limits, for activity is not a field but a line. This tenet is very old. We can see it in old teachers, but it is much clearer in the new. Some express it in their works as has been given here, and in other pedagogues it is evident in the content of their works. We can see this statement very well in Kerschensteiner or in the later well-known, American educator Dewey. Relying on this tenet, narrow specialization has been introduced into practice. It produces specialists who work in one direction and not *know-it-alls* who work in a broad field. The time has passed for professionals of so-called "universal knowledge." The time has come for narrow specialization which will rapidly send out into the world a highly productive and high-quality individual, into a single field.

The school first must set before itself a well-considered goal possible of realization and guide the children to this goal by a modern and noble method. Work itself is the marking of the goal for the individual and the realization of it with the help of knowledge and the will. It is said that in schools there is a wide gap between idea and practice. It is, therefore, necessary to cultivate the work but it is necessary always to give it a goal. At the same time, it is necessary to place that goal before the eyes of society, and this will increase respect for the school and will encourage its material support.

Turning to the question of tendencies, in this case, there are in mind tendencies only to certain disciplines. For example, a teacher gives to a student of mathematics a declamation to be made at some celebration. This student can solve very difficult mathematical problems but he cannot psychically understand the essence of a poetical work because he has no bent in this direction. Obviously, a poetical declamation by this student will be dull and wooden.

The moral tendencies in pedagogics are defined somewhat differently and we shall speak of them in other sections. Of course, if a teacher sees in a student any bad, immoral tendencies, he must not tolerate them but must, at all cost, struggle against them and try to root them out. But now comes the question: By what method? The teacher must choose the method, for the child represents a completely separate, closed world. The value of a teacher lies in the teacher's ability to enter, in a short time, into the soul of the child, establish himself, root out the weeds, and plant in their place useful grain. The teacher with a rod in his hand will teach a child even the most difficult subject, but he will never enter the soul of the child even after long years of teaching. The child, closed in himself, will perform the orders of the teacher as long as he fears him. Besides, it is important to remember that there are different temperaments, and each must be approached in a different way. First, it is necessary to recognize them in the children, and this can be done only by a qualified teacher who, in addition to his qualifications, also has the qualities of a good teacher.

Speaking of the calling of a teacher, each of us is convinced that one must be born a teacher. A thorough knowledge of his discipline and of the methods of teaching pupils are of great help to the teacher. However, the lectures of a teacher, who is a born pedagogue, rate high in helping pupils, especially when the lectures are lively and interesting.

Teaching and education are arts which cannot be totally acquired in school, for one must be born with certain gifts. A real teacher will never deliver a spiritless lecture; he will have every student under his control, for else he will be a dead figure who only performs certain mechanical functions. The work of a teacher under these latter circumstances can bring no proper satisfaction even to himself.

A person who has been born with the finer qualities of a teacher (even though he may not have attained the deep mechanical knowledge of teaching) will succeed by his method in transmitting the teaching material in so inspiring a fashion that the students not only will try to master the material thoroughly but will look with great attachment and respect on the person of the teacher. The highly intelligent teacher, with the inborn qualities necessary for the teaching profession, will never complain of a lack of discipline among his students for he will find suitable means for achieving his objective.

## Corporal Punishment

As soon as the method of Pestalozzi began to acquire natural rights in pedagogy, the number of incidences of physical punishments applied by teachers in the schools began to abate. The task of the school first is to introduce the method of so-called moral suasion, and with the help of this meritorious method, the teacher is able to accomplish much more than by compelling students to perform their duties by applying physical punishments. At all cost, in children must be awakened ambition, paired with a feeling of duty, which will be an internal force that at every moment will compel them to deal properly with their tasks. In this manner, children will have the possibility of developing their ideas and guiding them in their own direction.

The unreasonable sternness of parents or of teachers never turns out for good, for such parents and teachers lose their authority in the eyes of their children. And, in a large degree, their children and pupils lose confidence in them. Physical punishments greatly blunt the minds of children and, furthermore, develop stubbornness and even brutality. They kill ambition and meritorious feelings. They are opposed to the spirit of the meritorious development of personality. Physical punishments are an old resource of incapable teachers who not only did not know how to teach and educate but who probably actually did not want to undertake this work seriously. There have been cases where children have been crippled for life because of corporal punishments and have gazed with deep sorrow and contempt at their parents or teachers as the perpetrators of their misfortune. If the occasion actually arises that no argument can penetrate the mind and the taut nerves of a child can be quieted only by corporal punishment, it must be as a last resort and never the first. At the same time, there is the right to demand from parents or teachers that at this moment they be guided by the criteria of healthy reason and not give rein to their exasperated nerves.

The ultimate desire and need that perfects the qualifications of a proper teacher is sympathy. It is born of understanding children, comprehending their desires and efforts. These qualities of understanding and comprehending are so highly valuable for a teacher, for, if they are not included in the program of teaching and education, one cannot assume that the result of the teacher's labor will achieve a properly high level. A true teacher is one who has an inborn tendency toward the calling to be a teacher. He has a ceaseless desire to continue training himself, for he constantly feels the need for progress in carrying out the mission of a teacher.

To insure a proper result, a teacher must dedicate himself fully to his calling of teaching and educating. This is understood and felt at once by his pupils and, at that moment, there is born in them sympathy for their teacher which will simultaneously guarantee their future high intellectual and moral level. By securing the sympathy of the children, the teacher is able to develop in the educational process the ability (1) To teach the children how to develop all their good inclinations. — The teacher then is the active link between the children and the teaching material. — (2) To teach the students how to live, for life is a great craft which possesses the keys to reality and truth. The lives of the children especially are hard, because they do not have a great deal of experience. The teacher must teach the children to observe phenomena, to find their causation, and to indicate the results of their action.

## The Health of the Teacher

The next important factor is health. Teaching is hard work. It very often undermines the health of even physically strong teachers. In every healthy body there is a healthy soul that incorporates joy and an eagerness to work. The teacher must, of necessity, be optimistic for the pupils will then share his conviviality; the school will be a second home, and learning will be a pleasure.

Certainly, each of us have had the opportunity in life to meet teachers who casually must have chosen the teaching profession without having the slightest inner and spiritual contact with it. It is exactly in this case that we perceive a gloomy figure, dark as the night, indifferent, automatic, and inaccessible — the figure of a teacher-pedagogue, educator and esthete all embodied in one figure. Instead of influencing them through meritorious conduct, his professional knowledge and his exemplary life, he attempts to exercise authority over his pupils, keeping himself at a distance from them. Such a teacher wants to accomplish his work by his taciturnity, his inaccessibility and full detachment especially from his pupils. Yet, no one can succeed on an artificial road, for whatever the distance he holds, every one senses it involuntarily, differentiates between the intelligence of the teacher and his "meritorious" conduct, so that the teacher's personal emphasis of his own ego appears excessive.

A cheerful but natural relationship never deters obedience. This natural optimism comes primarily from good health and, therefore, the teacher must be physically strong. When it is a question of psychic values, the teacher must stand on a high moral level, for he is a builder of characters. The teacher must be inspired by his work. It must keep him spiritually fresh, for it is the first cause of his uninterrupted intellectual and spiritual growth. For his work to have proper success, it is not enough to draw knowledge from books, but he must first of all draw it from his philosophy of life. His experiences are much greater than knowledge which is found in books. A philosophy of life is found even in folklore, and by knowledge of this, at least, to a certain degree, the teacher can know the child better. Knowing a child is quite a difficult problem which not every teacher can solve.

## Knowledge of the Physical Nature of the Students

The first of the main obligations of a teacher is to know in what conditions every child lives. The teacher must take part in the physical activities of the students. The educator must first turn his attention to the physical dexterity of the students and point out to the parents the way for the better physical development of their children. Knowledge and active participation also automatically make the teacher their guide in those activities which the young consider as bestowing the highest prestige.

Knowledge of sports gives the teacher the opportunity to observe the conduct of the young on the playing fields with respect to the attitude of the students to the rules of the game, to the umpire, the opponents, the environment, and to the intended objective. Through all the reflexes of the students, the teacher can analyze the temperaments of his students, their will power, and even their intelligence. The properly knowledgeable cooperation of the teacher with the students in sports raises the authority of the teacher and educator, and he will enjoy the sympathy of the young people. In this, he must have strength of will and make certain that the young carry out his orders and instructions. However, in assigning the work, the teacher must indicate the goal to the students.

To educate means to teach how to live well, wisely, and graciously. The educator must himself, first of all, know life, must first know how to adapt himself to its various manifestations, must know how to conduct himself, and must influence life.

To know life, to love life, and to know how to manage it are the chief qualities of a teacher. The educator who buries himself in one field loses sight of life and so cannot prepare others for it. By this burial, the author means that the teacher shows interest only in his subject which he constantly expounds in school. A shoemaker, chauffeur, or other artisan can have one trade, and only one trade, but a person active in society cannot permit himself this narrowness, and this applies all the more to an educator. The teacher must take part in the most diverse manifestations of life or else he is threatened with dry routine and the deadening of his work.

A not-less-characteristic feature is pedantry. It should be permeated with the life of the modern school. Very often, this pedantry transforms a pedagogue into an automatic, petty, and dull book-worm both toward the children and the subjects of instruction. In general, when it is a question of each calling, it can be said that a person at the time of aspiring to a profession recognizes first the individual and social content of his whole life and connects his personal life with the existence of the entire universe. So in every calling, there are, to some degree, solemn chords. In taking a particular burden on his shoulders, the person sees not only the beginning but also the end of his life's road.

## Our Idea of an Educator

The pedagogue, in our conception, is a permanent student; he not only forms others but he must constantly continue to form himself. Participation in the pedagogical process keeps him always young. Every child by its individuality seems to introduce corrections in his pedagogical principles and methods. Furthermore, in crossing the threshold of the school, the pedagogue introduces into the life of the school a certain degree of the life which is beyond its walls. While the pedagogue of the old school synthesized untouchability and detachment in himself, the pedagogue facing the future is completely different; he takes part in each pedagogical act and transmits his good attributes to his audience.

Present social development is proceeding along the line of the greatest democratization of culture and is breaking all the barriers between the school and life. Tolstoy foresaw that the future school probably would change completely its views and become a museum, a unique paradise. Such a school will affect pedagogical selection most advantageously and will raise the profession of teaching to the level of its calling.

## THE SOCIAL HERITAGE IN EDUCATION

*Historical Sketch*

In speaking about heritage, there are constantly two kinds in mind: (1) Biological; (2) Sociological. Both have brought man to the height of present culture and civilization. A person profits from all its achievements from the first moment of his life. He adds his own achievements and passes on the totality to his descendants. The understanding of the importance and meaning of society is imperative for every person, for on the degree of his understanding will depend the level of his spiritual and physical values and his future life-career. In the general use of the terms culture, civilization and social heritage are synonyms. In an accurate discussion can be found a difference between them, but this does not change their real essence.

In studying social heritage, one comes to the conclusion that social heritage stems from the time when a person was physically and psychically extremely different from modern man. Primitive man was capable of such "intelligent" achievements as to fasten bits of sharp stone to pieces of wood so that with the aid of these implements he could better protect himself against wild beasts and more easily secure food.

The life of primitive man did not differ very much from the life of animals. Man lived that way through various periods. In accordance with discoveries by man during those periods, modern man has given various names to those periods. During the three periods named Eolithic, Paleolithic, and Neolithic man used only stone and wood. The ages of metals followed, and they were accompanied by a rapid physical and spiritual development of man.

Primitive man used only stone and wood for more than a half million years, which period received the name of the Stone Age. This was followed by the metal ages of copper and bronze which began approximately nine thousand years before the birth of Christ. Approximately nine hundred years before the birth of Christ began the Iron Age, which contributed most to the development of civilized man. Iron helped him to cultivate fields properly and to build houses. It was most useful for weapons, which to a great degree safeguarded the life of man. Later, the exchange of goods was initiated which gave rise to trade. This, in turn, disseminated the achievements of the culture over our whole sphere.

The man of this period certainly understood the advantages of social life. He built settlements and strongly fortified them. It was this period which defined man as a rational animal, and this he owes to the common efforts of society.

## Communal Environment and Education

The communal environment is responsible primarily for social heritage. It assumes the responsibility for all forms of communal life as customs, fashion, morals, and, above all, language. The most important elements in social life, however, are ideas and public opinion.

A man adapts himself to the ideas of other people. Ideas of those, naturally, who are able to influence society, for he sees only in these ideas the possibility for improving his own existence. Furthermore, public opinion is the chief support of social progress. It is subject to great changes. Public opinion often considers even completely natural modes of life as needless.

The rules of government in democratic states depend on public opinion to a great degree. Not less dependent on public opinion is the education of the young in schools. Hence, when we read the papers and each day find in them news of street crimes of school children such as robberies, fights and murders, judgment must first fall upon society, for on it depends the mode of education of their children in the schools. It can make the laws more rigorous, just as the present, mild laws were once made. Thus, the future of the young generation also must depend upon the conscience of society.

## The Environment and Education

When one considers the theory of Weissman, one certainly comes to the conclusion that it (if not in whole then at least in part) agrees with our views on the question. Certainly, every one of us agrees that changes in the form of improvements of the human race confirm the importance of this theory, for every following generation uses and really has as a base for further development all the achievements of preceding generations. This applies not only to intellectual capacities, but on these achievements also depends in large degree the moral and psychic development of all later generations.

Another important factor on which the improvement of the race largely depends is the environment in which the younger generation grows and is educated. Every young generation inherits from its predecessors not only all natural qualities but even special tendencies, even tendencies to the construction of machines, industry, trade, systems and means. It further inherits social ideals either as a whole or perhaps at times in a changed form, but mainly it inherits language and customs. All conditions which are the product of civilization, and which are found on every road along which all coming generations pass, can, in a general sense, be called, social qualities. They include all intellectual capabilities, beliefs, customs, laws, languages, attachments to the family and society, and everything in which a person is born and through which he is educated. History itself has shown that the children of immoral parents will often have immoral tendencies which can be removed only by a favorable education and in a moral environment.

There are territories inhabited by the descendants of old pirates. Although many centuries have passed, the present inhabitants of these territories still have a great tendency to raiding expeditions, and this is only because they settled in an unpopulated territory and, therefore, had no one from whom they could have inherited a cultural mode of life.

Relying on the reports of various charitable organizations, it can be said that not less than eighty-five per cent of the children of morally unsound parents become reliable individuals and model citizens if they have suitable surroundings and a good system of education.

Every nation, and even every child, has its own sentiments, moral and artistic ideals, traditions and customs which it must transmit at all costs to the coming generations. Everybody must act to improve humanity, beginning with improving family life. The family will reflect on society. Thus, our goal in education will most quickly and most constantly be achieved. First, there must be the fostering of morality and all our inherited values in our

family, for these are the bases of every healthy people and dominat·
ing nation. But, if we wish to improve life in our families, we must
completely separate family life from the life of the street, otherwise,
parents will not be able to give their children a proper education.

Developing the problem of the education of children, it is strange
how parents can be so shortsighted as to think only of the material
well-being of their children and pay no attention to their moral
values. After all, the chief task of education is to improve character
and to make it solid. At the same time, the education of the
street goes along completely opposite lines. Hence, when parents
allow their children to spend whole days on the street, they are
fostering the struggle of the two worlds in the souls of their
children, and in this struggle the world of the street usually wins,
for it better suits young people.

When we turn to the question of inherited achievements, they
must be the basis of further development. The natural process lies
not only on the change of forms but also in the continuous dis-
covery of something new. These new discoveries, however, must
have a harmonious relationship to the discoveries of their predecessors, for only then can it be a natural process. Radical changes,
in any sector whatever, do not bring good results. As proof that
these statements are objective we can convince ourselves when we
consider modern music or art.

Prior to a few decades ago, music was isolated from even the
slightest discordance, for at the time this lack of harmony was
considered something unnatural. Lack of harmony was opposed
to the feeling of the soul of a man and so was avoided in all
creativeness. In the same manner, art of that period did not seek
beauty in the products of the Stone Age, for artists believed that
it was a degradation to take subjects from a period when man
was not, in the exact meaning of the word, a person wherein
animal instincts prevailed. Returning to present day music, it can
be said that even in the jungles now we will not hear less-har-
monious music, and the dance of youth constantly stresses the
sexual side of human nature.

In analyzing the years in which this lack of harmony in music
began to acquire a basic right, it is very easy to find that it broke
through a trail on which later followed lack of harmony in the
relationship of children toward their parents, in marital life, of
pupils toward teachers, and at every step this lack of harmony

is now considered as being fully valuable and worthy of fostering.

Art at this time is seeking something new, for it wishes to be original, wishes to begin a new school or even a new era and, instead of rising, it is day-by-day descending into the depths of the Stone Age. It can be developed in our works with great originality if we try to devote ourselves to examining the nature of the world as well as the nature of man. It is important also, not to forget, that the nature of man consists not only of a body but a soul as well, and man must give it the opportunity to grow and develop to its full potentiality.

### *Tradition as the Basis of Education*

It is known that an innate capacity and circumstance are the factors which together produce outstanding individuals. Inherited capability is the main and more permanent cause, since the second factor, i.e., circumstances, is artificial and, therefore, the quality of these factors is always dependent upon ourselves.

The family and the school are the two institutions on which the social order depends; their task must also be to provide society with outstanding individuals by creating favorable circumstances, which is the second factor necessary for the development of an outstanding personality. For the family and the school to be healthy factors, they must have their definitely marked goal and ideals, based on tradition, which must be regarded as something most real and penetrating. Looking at history, or even in analyzing the present peoples, everybody sees that only those nations stand high morally, culturally, and materially which have strong ties with tradition. These peoples try only to improve every sector, i.e., to adapt it to the needs of the day, but they never break with the achievements of their ancestors. The school must also be constructed on the continuation of tradition. Its task must be to find the approach which will make the old achievements useful and practically beneficial today and in the future.

Modern education has as its task the transmission to the young descendants all of the marks of the cultural and spiritual life of their forefathers. The school must make every effort to secure the good will and respect of the younger people, for all the values of society which enrich it so greatly spiritually raise it to a high level.

Spiritual values and religious, national, and family celebrations indicate a great cultural inheritance of a given people. Anniversaries and birthdays in each people have a definite coloring which are marked by special ceremonies and even kinds of gifts. The clothing which people wear at various celebrations depends on the occasion. The definite rules set for betrothals, weddings, small receptions, and even funerals — as to clothing, food, and everything else — are almost natural laws which lie deep in the soul of every cultural people, and its future generations must ever preserve the greatest values handed down by their ancestors.

This law of natural popular mores and customs is so neglected that there is some doubt that the following generation will not in any way or on any occasion manifest the precious values of their own people. The school must at every opportunity emphasize the importance and value of all the cultural achievements of a given people, so that the youth might receive spiritual nourishment from the healthy roots of their ancestors. Such education will raise his own spiritual worth in the eyes of the child and will bid him not to stain the nobility and beauty of the achievements of his forefathers by a light and frivolous life.

### The Cause of the Loss of Character

The social position of society depends first upon the character of the individuals who create it. At the present time, which is considered a period of moral crisis, the problem of the training of character is becoming even more vital in view of the tremendous growth of every kind of immorality and the criminality which are its consequences. This unpleasant situation cannot fail to disturb society for it primarily threatens our replacements — the young. No one will deny the fact that a great number of the young, beginning with children of the lowest grades of the elementary schools, are living and growing up in a morass of immoralism in the broadest sense of the word. Reading in the press of cases of this kind and evaluating them, we come to the conclusion that this spiritual chaos is becoming widespread, that it is passing into the final evil, i.e., where everyone considers this phenomenon unconditionally bad, but no one has the courage to speak up and do something about it.

The question now arises: What is the cause of this moral decline? The first source is the present day family. We cannot blame the children whose entire day is spent in education on the street. They do not hear the language of their mother, for the mother is working on the night shift, sleeps during the day, and is satisfied that the children are on the street, for she can rest. The father comes from work in a factory and eats quickly so as not to be late for work at another place. In a word, one overtime overlaps another. So, days pass after days. At the same time, when the balance is growing in the father's bankbook, the children also are growing and, in talking with them, you can scarcely recognize them. They are permeated with the *bon-ton* of the street. This appears not only in their speech but also in their movements and even in their looks.

Question: Is it a stupid or a sensible calculation on the one hand to work until utterly exhausted in order to acquire more property for the children and, at the same time, deprive the same children of what parents are bound by written and unwritten law to provide, an education above all?

Here we must warn the parents that by working thusly and by not bringing up their children, they are doing a great wrong — in the first place — to themselves, to their children, and to society.

Next to the home, the school is another important factor in character building since, after the home, the children spend most of their time at school. Indeed, if schools were able to give the children proper training, they would take at least one-half of the burden of education off the parents. However, in some modern schools, instead of being true teachers, some teachers have become mere instructors. They are only concerned with the subjects for which they get paid, without taking an interest in real education. This is the only explanation of existing conditions, for how else could we justify the acts of some dissolute pupils of some lay-schools who, from the ninth or tenth year of age, smoke in the presence of teachers and use profane language which shocks the ears. No one will call this a figment of the imagination; it is enough to spend a little time in the vicinity of such a school to find out that this is the plain truth.

*It behooves us here to note with respect the methods used in parochial schools. Instruction, and particularly training, is basically different than in the above described lay-schools.* There are very few noted instances of pupils of parochial schools being members of street gangs or being candidates for inmates of correctional institutions; this is due mainly to the fact that in parochial schools instruction and education are inextricably bound together, and a teacher is an educator, something that for some reason cannot be accomplished within some public school systems. This is not the fault of pedagogy as a science. Going through the works of ancient and modern pedagogues, both theoreticians as well as practitioners, the author never found a hint that an educator, for the sake of entertaining the pupils, would advise them to smoke, play cards, or, otherwise, suggest the use of narcotics to enrich their bodily experiences. If such is the case, we can assert as a fact that pedagogy, in the true sense of the word, has been shelved and will emerge from the dust into the school buildings only after legislators begin to show an interest in it. When the latter begin to understand the basic idea of education, curb the unwarranted freedom of young people, and replace it with rules of discipline, the idea of education will benefit and grow and contribute to the healthy growth of the nation.

In defending the idea of education, teachers always must bear in mind the above-noted heritage, and deal with different children who have different inherited backgrounds, and hence adopt an individual approach to each child. They must also consider the inborn nature of the child which comes endowed with certain qualities; this nature has a major effect on the results of our efforts. Mental and physical development, the character mold, and the state of interests and tendencies fully depend on inherently existing capabilities in a person which contribute to his development in one direction or another. Therefore, the first act facing the teacher is to recognize the kind of aptitudes which the child has grown into by nature, because this is like an investment capital which the teacher must capably manipulate so that it would bring visible profits within a short time. If the teacher does not make these necessary observations and conclusions, he will soon have no ground on which to erect his pedagogical activities.

The original nature of every child is based on its nervous system, and is largely inherited, i.e., every person inherits it to a degree from his ancestors. Thus, most human traits are inherited from ancestors, and this is what makes children differ from one another even in early childhood. Hence, the teacher cannot train children according to a set pattern for all, but must approach children as individuals.

The teachers must be guided by the child's inherited natural traits in order to develop them and should never act contrary to their tendencies. The nature of a child is not a blank sheet of paper, nor is it, of course, a clean slate, but the genes have already marked it, and it is up to the parents and teachers to develop the existing traits with appropriate teaching and instruction.

The inherited effect in the formation of an individual is so deep that we cannot immediately fathom it; nevertheless, the teacher must make every effort to learn of its extent and simultaneously seek practical means to direct the course of possible negative inherited traits toward a positive goal. Education is not capable of changing all the traits which a child possesses by inheritance, it can only set a direction for them. The responsibility for negative traits in a child lies with the parents or even with more remote antecedents whose physical or psychical lives were faulty. However, it is not an important concern of the teacher to delve into the origins of the negative traits, this being rather the province of biologists. The teacher merely should investigate the quality of these traits in order to find the proper means of leading the negative traits onto a desired path.

## THE ROLE OF THE WILL IN THE EDUCATIONAL PROCESS

*The Psychology of the Will*

Psychology shows that the psychic life is composed of various processes, each of which includes a certain number of intellectual, emotional, and volitional elements. In every psychic action, all these elements take part, although there is the difference that in one psychic act one element takes the major, most evident place, and, again, in another psychic action, this place is taken by another element. In every psychic action there appear simultaneous, intellectual, and volitional elements, that mutually supplement each other. Even at those moments when a person is in a most exasperated state, his mind still functions somewhat. Hence, here the intellectual element appears. Although these elements appear together in every psychic action, there is always a difference between them which guides the psyche.

Objectivity is a positive side of thinking, for the aim of thinking is to ascertain the truth. In contrast, subjectivity is an erroneous process of thought. This difference between the elements plays a large role, for it turns our psyche on the objective world and, depending upon the quality of its direction, our judgments are more or less true. As regards feelings, they are nothing but the purely internal experiences of every person which are made evident externally, i.e., on the face of the person or through his movements, because of fear, joy, sorrow, anger. Feelings are exposed when our thinking is directed toward an object. Therefore, all our feelings depend on the quality of the object. The object is only the cause of joy, but joy and sorrow in themselves are our inner experience. The process of thinking and of passing judgments must not be based upon feelings, for then they will be false, i.e., subjective.

A further important mark of the will is its activity. Action immediately indicates the most noticeable form of the will, whereas, contemplation was primarily the most important form of thinking. During our thinking, we become conscious of the action which the external world has directed toward us. Upon this cognizance, feeling is born within us and we simultaneously register joy or sorrow as a reaction to the action of the external world. However, in the process of our will, there appears something entirely opposite to the preceding, and that is: we act on the external world with the purpose of changing it in some way.

### Definition of the Will

In the narrow sense of the word the will denotes an action which is under the full control and guidance of the intellectual powers. This capacity for deliberation and defining is an action in which the end of the action is foreseen and even contrived. In the broader sense the will can be defined as containing the entire interior life and manifestations or the sum of all strivings which also include all stimuli, instincts, and reflexes, that is, to the extent to which they appear. The will also manifests itself in controlling our feelings as well as in guiding our intellectual life.

In analyzing the broader and narrower definition, it cannot be said that control fully defined the term will. The will, as well as the deliberate causation of an action which has its own basis, possesses its potentials in all the elements of the psychic life which is mentioned in the broader definition. The will is a broad term. It must include the fullness of all psychic conditions on which the will is fully dependent, issuing orders and instructions; for all external actions must be in harmony with the internal disposition of the individual, if they are aimed at a planned and previously deliberated performance of the actions.

One must understand the importance of the will as the total reaction of the individual to all forces which act upon it, or, also, as the reaction which comes from the most internal psychic impulses or instinctive strivings. The will always takes part in a conscious act. The making of judgments is an essential form of the work of reason, for it includes the center of all actions and their synthesis. Therefore, in every judgment, as for example, "A" is subject to "B," "A" represents a point in which a recognizable act is concentrated, when "B" represents an idea which is connected with "A" during the very act of our judgment. The act of the will is, therefore, essential.

The will is not the same type of reality as capability, which is independent and which cooperates with the other factors of our thought, but it is one of the essential features of the characteristics of the wholeness of life or thinking. The most important thing in understanding the will is that the will is the center of the conscious establishment of a goal. Further, the will contains, at its core, elementary movements in the form of reflexes, impulses, and instincts. It usually is spurred to an action by the lack of balance in the physiological and, still more, in the psychical state of a person. But the activity of a person goes far beyond the boundaries of the physiological or even the psychical equilibrium, because a person reacts not only to external but also to internal causes, although very often this is not conscious. Then, the action comes not from the person himself but from the power which has been placed in him (the need for eating, the need for speaking, etc.). Consciousness only comes to the person after he has gained definite experience.

But experience is not everything for, it also exists in animals. Yet, the animal is not able to perform an action which would be comparable to the reasonable actions of a person. In this case, man as a rational animal stands high above an animal, for he has set as a goal all those omissions which nature itself could not make up and strives to fill them with the aid of his experience. Not only can a man become aware of his needs, but he can also decide in advance all the paths by which he can achieve his purpose. At the same time, a person is able to concentrate his experience in a few impressions and pass over others or, in general, pay no attention to them. Attention, as such, is a true directing and concentrating of the psyche on certain phenomena or subjects.

The emotions also have great significance for they arouse attention. Beside the emotions, attention is stirred by interest and by impressions which evoke joy, sorrow, or other experiences. We can also divide attention into voluntary and involuntary. The first is natural only to man, the second to both man and animals. In animals involuntary attention is due very often to habits as well as to external and internal causes. Voluntary attention is natural only to man, for his characteristic feature is his conscious striving for a previously planned goal. It plays a great role in all higher, human, psychic processes, for its activity lies in the combination of shapes or even of elements which have remained in our con-

sciousness through the processes of acceptance. The artist or
musician employs a special form of attention during his inspired
creativity which is natural only to man and only in the higher
stages of his development. This kind of attention has something
in common with involuntary attention, because such a person
does not have to make great efforts and, therefore, the process of
experience moves along quite a smooth path. But not every person
can acquire this kind of attention. This kind of attention can
appear only after voluntary attention has been active, at least,
for some time previously.

The prerequisite for every process of the will is a desire, but
the process of the will begins with a consciousness of need. A
person has many desires, but they are often not stable, are
ephemeral, and leave no trace behind them. Longings, however,
are a higher stage of development of the will and, for a time, at
least, they remain in the conscious awareness of a person. Very
often, the volitional process comes up against a situation which
offers no solution. This usually happens when the person hesitates,
and this condition of his psyche is called a struggle of motives.
The significance of motives in the psychic process is very evident,
for they are essentially the motive powers of our consciousness.
Thinking and emotions play a great role in the struggle of motives.
Such a struggle of motives does not last equally long in every
person, and a decision is reached eventually.

The importance of the will, in individual life as well as in
social life, stems from the importance of its actions, which it can
direct in various directions. In every individual, the will is the
source of character and accomplishment; it has the mind under
its disposal, works with it or permits it to wither. It realizes all
the capabilities with which nature has endowed us through inheritance. In the community, the will is a very responsible factor,
for on it depend customs, laws, and morals. It includes the instinct
of self-preservation, or the so-called first law of nature; it assures
the existence of the individual and society.

Every creature attempts to live the life for which it is best
fitted. This natural disposition makes itself evident by various
stimuli and their clearly defined actions. A person also desires
to live the life of a person in the full sense of the word. The
life of a person in differentiation from the life of other creatures
is reasonable and historical; in it a person always finds the place

and time to practice all human intellectual forces and virtues. A person wishes to do everything that is in the natural order and which coincides with his development. We must consider all relations of man-to-man as actions which our life imposes on us, and our humanity will better reveal itself in our methods of approach and the application of our ego to all these natural activities.

We must not regard as less natural the relations of children to their parents, of pupils to teachers. The result which comes from these relationships brings great satisfaction to an intelligent man, for then the person gains conviction, and this conviction begets in him a new desire to live with his brothers as a brother, and among members of a community as a member of a community. In the teacher, there is produced also a desire to teach as long as possible so as to pass on as many of his achievements as possible to his audience.

The training of the will is the most important action of education. This is the actual education of one's self, and the chief goal of training the will is to make it capable of holding all our instincts under its control and of guiding them, so that their activity will not be haphazard but will develop from the stimuli of reason. The second need for the training of the will comes from the importance of making judgments. A trained will will never permit the body to execute ill-defined reflexes, for every reflex has its own goal. Training in self-control is the highest quality of training reason. Therefore, the family and school, where the will receives its best training, must teach the will to make use of the judgments of reason. It is improper to speak of the emancipation of children, or even of young persons, because their will is not fully mature and yet cannot be guided by all its manifestations. Education is not a process of guess-work but an accurately defined work which rests on fundamental principles.

### *Our Unused Talents*

The will is the greatest human capability; it is all human thought in action, it is the internal motor, the stronghold of all human powers and capabilities. Nevertheless, the will cannot directly create or reveal these powers, for they are the product of the factors of development, inheritance, environment, and uninterrupted labor. These powers usually are revealed quite accidentally or of necessity.

Activate all our capabilities more-or-less skillfully. This depends upon our experiences. What we usually do, is less than we could do, for we naturally spare ourselves, and this restraint we can only overcome in special cases such as tests and in other unexpected circumstances, where we often surprisingly give more of ourselves than we had thought possible and are amazed at the source of our knowledge. This self-conservation is lesser in some, greater in others. Darwin said that people are differentiated more by effort and industry than by capacity, which every person possesses in a greater or lesser degree. In all people, the capacity for intellectual development is much greater than we usually expect. Here we could easily apply the Biblical parable of the talents: one is born with five talents, one with two, and the third with one talent; the used talents multiply, and the unused are left unchanged and undeveloped. The person whom someone has induced to use his talents should consider himself fortunate. But even greater joy should be felt by the individual who has not only been induced to use his talents but who has been taught how to develop them.

It is quite certain that a large number of geniuses are born in the world. Unfortunately, no one knows about them, and they leave this world as people of the lowest class, only because there was no power to discover their talents and show the way to develop them. One can take as examples inventors, physicians, engineers, and other professional people. Many of them were unnoticed individuals, but favorable circumstances revealed their deeply hidden talents, and people came forth who indicated the direction and method of their development.

An easy life, a comfortable life, will never arouse slumbering powers in a person. They are aroused only by a hard life which arouses all the latent or slumbering powers in a person and bids them be active to find ways and methods so that a person cannot only preserve himself in life but can also make life easy and pleasant. Often, in our lives, we have met people whose fathers were rich and their comfortable lives did not give their children the opportunity to arouse their latent capacities for which reason their children remained incompletely developed for life and were not fit for life. At the same time, we have met children of poor people, artisans, whose lives were hard and uncomfortable, whose circumstances compelled them in early youth to find ways to live and to try to expect something better. These children of unintelligent parents very often have reached high positions, and only because of their great working ability and vitality.

The schools very often make this mistake for they try to make life in the school as easy as possible, comfortable, and irresponsible. The chief task of the school must be to develop self-control in the children and to harden them so well for life that no difficulties on their life's path will be unsurmountable for them. Such an education acquaints the student with his intellectual, psychic, and physical powers and develops his self-confidence and responsibility. It is true that strength of will is also dependent on heredity. Thus, one man from birth has a greater power of self-control, and a second has the same capacity in a lesser degree. Yet, in every person, this capacity acquires active strength only with the aid of development. This is one of the chief factors which makes every person more or less valuable.

It is a fact shown by science and the practice of life that all our inherited possibilities can be increased or lost, but constant effort is required to develop them. The teachers must believe in the power of development and the possibility of a change for the better through the path of development, for these ideas will stimulate them to action, and their first successes will give them the desire to develop their hidden talents and at the same time to control them, to guide them to that goal which they consider is the best.

### The Power of the Will in Education

Speaking of the will, we at the same time understand the term will as a part of individuality. "Individuality," moreover, is a synonym of the will. It is not correct to define will by the terms capability and endowment, for by these terms we understand such endowments as reason, memory, and emotions.

All acts of consciousness are related mutually and form an organic unity, a conscious personality. Will is only the name of a fact, a factor of which is consciousness. Consciousness is knowledge, it is the agent of the senses. It establishes our individuality. Will is the active form of consciousness, and to it we owe the establishment of our individuality.

In accurately classifying the terms, we note the difference between personality and individuality. A personality is a full consciousness that includes various phases of recognition, energy, and stimuli. Individuality is a motive or a phase of the will of personality.

Personality is a concrete term, but individuality is an abstract term. In the common use of these terms, personality and individuality are synonyms, but in the term individuality, we can see the intentions, actions, and character of the person.

With the help of the will, we either develop or neglect our capabilities which we received from our ancestors by way of inheritance. A gifted person has the power to broaden and improve all his capabilities to the limits that he wishes. In this case the quality of the person and the quality of his future life depend exclusively upon the strength of his will. The strength of will, in this case, is most important, for it permits even lesser gifts by inheritance to be broadened, and unfavorable circumstances to be changed for the better. But we cannot create new capabilities by the strength of our will; we can only broaden them, develop them, and make them useful to us.

Our thoughts stimulate us to action, and action through repetition becomes a habit, and all our habits produce our character.

In addition, different circumstances and actions lead us to our final achievements and thus create our fate.

> "Our character is that trait by the strength of which we are what we are, and our fate has given us everything we possess. Character and fate are not shaped separately to each person, but in the process of existence they establish themselves, and this is where inheritance and circumstances play a great role. The quality of our fate depends firstly on ourselves, that is, on the strength of our will. The weaker the will, the weaker and the less sure the path of our life. We can have even very fine, high, and realizable intentions, but if we have no strong will, everything begins in us with intentions and plans and ends the same way. For the will to be strong, we must try to overcome all obstacles on the path of our life from our youngest years and never avoid them, for the latter is the custom of people of weak character. Will, in the strict sense of the word, is not given to a person at the

moment of his birth, but it is fashioned gradually on the base of involuntary movements. This process of forming the will must be well understood by a teacher so that he can correctly guide the education of the young generation."[1]

He must begin to harden the will of the children from their early childhood. This is a thorny road in rearing, for all the movements of a child are impulses, reflexes, and instincts which the child performs without the least consciousness. With the development of reason, the unconscious movements of a child become more and more defined, for then his reason approximately marks his course. Thus, these movements gradually are more-and-more perfected, for the child daily acquires more experience. It is in these first movements that the character of the child begins to develop. The child is moulded first by the environment in which he grows and is reared. As soon as the child rises to his feet, he feels the need to be guided by motives of a moral order to the degree which is required of him. Then the child distinguishes a good action from a bad, feels the reproaches of conscience, shows confusion, blushes, and even is ashamed. In this little child, already, even by these signs, everyone will notice that he is a reasonable being, for he has a full consciousness of his actions as well as moral responsibility. To justify himself, he tries to find the same evil actions in others.

The quality of his character is influenced by the surroundings in which the child is reared. The environment, the living world, and examples of older persons are the mould into which, with great difficulty, at first, we place the still undeveloped soul of the child, but a suitable environment makes this process less difficult, and eventually the conduct of the child takes the form which his surroundings and his rearers give it.

With the development of the criteria of reason, impulsiveness weakens and the will acquires strength. In analyzing the child, from the first weeks of its existence in the world, we see that the first movements of the infant are impulses and instincts, but, later with the development of reason, there comes also an aware-

1. Vashchenko, Hryhoriy, *Vykhovannya Voli i Kharakteru*, London, Caplin and Co., Press Ltd. Croy don, 1952, Part I., p. 29.

ness of these movements, and still later the infant becomes aware of their consequences.

In a somewhat older child, a struggle of motives arises as a result of which he begins to master his impulsiveness and with every day guides his movements better. The older children, those of approximately school age, display definite intolerance which is one of the forms of the instinct of self-defense. This intolerance in children very often passes into habits which slow the development of the reasoning powers, and the child could become an asocial type. In this case, the school must take upon itself the responsibility of not allowing the child to continue developing his intolerance. It can be overcome successfully with the help of theory and practice.

Following the period of the younger school years comes the period of adolescence. This is usually the child's years from 12 to 16. This period, Prof. H. Vashchenko calls the period of subjective interests. The nature of an adolescent is in broad outlines similar to the nature of the child of pre-school age. A peculiar characteristic of the adolescent is that he can become aware of himself and even consider himself a famous personality. The thoughts of the adolescent are usually crowded with fantastic dreams, which rest chiefly on a sexual basis. The adolescent believes that he must not live a humdrum life, but that he must seek adventures in the world so that he can become known and famous.

At this period one should examine the environment in which the adolescent is growing up, for on this environment greatly depends the future character of the child. An unhealthy environment and immoral literature result in the character of the adolescent acquiring an erotic coloring. On the other hand, if, during this period of the child, the parents and school turn attention to his environment and do not allow him to grow up loosely, but exert efforts to improve the conditions in which he is growing up, the romanticism which stupefies the young mind can take a quite different direction — it will then favor the development of courage and incline the adolescent at all costs to achieve, at least, some elevated ideals.

Confirmation of this can be seen in the almost daily news items in the press where we read that adolescents reared in the streets group themselves into robber bands and attack shops and passersby, which makes it difficult for the police to repress them. This transitional age is the most difficult in the process of education. It ends when sexual equilibrium has been established, which is the commencement of the period of young adulthood.

In this period romanticism and an inclination to dreaming still remain, but their manifestations are not so strong as in adolescents, for young adults think more how to build a better future for themselves, what calling to pursue. Those young adults who are gifted with special talents find their choice of profession very easy, but it is more difficult for those who have no special talents, for at this time they undergo great vacillation because they cannot decide which profession to choose. They very often change their course, for it seems to them that one profession does not please them and that another will be better. This change in their choice of professional and technical preparation can be explained by the fact that the young adult rationalizes that many future difficult problems await him, and, in order to solve them in some manner, he must find the most appropriate occupation which will give him spiritual satisfaction as well as a material means of livelihood.

The age of young adulthood can also be called the age of the appearance of creativeness. In this age, talents appear most clearly. The young adult puts forth all his efforts to deepen himself and to understand questions in the field of philosophy, which the professional philosopher himself avoids because of the unconquerable difficulties of their solution.

A great problem with this age is that it still retains traces of the adolescence period. The young adult has not yet acquired firm stability and, in addition, still possesses the sensitivity of the adolescent, all of which is confronted with the great demands of life, and as a result a spiritual breakdown often occurs.

In analyzing various periods in the life of a person, it can be safely said that the period of young adulthood is the most beautiful period of life, and whoever wisely takes advantage of this period will remain spiritually young until his death.

*Work as the Chief Means of Forming Will and Character*

Every activity comes from the will, for this is shown by the entire system of movements, the source of which is the will. But all persons do not have the same strength of will, and so the quality of actions is different.

The exercise of the will requires the emotions of need and desire, and these, to a large degree, depend on the condition and age of the person, on the climate, and his social position. There are also various forms of activity which are dependent upon the intellectual and physical development of the person. But whatever be the pattern of his activity, it still gives a certain form to the person, and usually according to his activity, he assumes one form or another. Physical work gives one form to a person, and intellectual work forms a person on another pattern. Yet the important thing is that the form of the person is dependent upon his will. In other words, "As you sow, so shall you reap."

Work falls under various fields and subfields. The main divisions of labor are intellectual and physical. But these divisions have a conditional character, for there are callings where intellectual work includes many elements of physical work. The reverse can be true, too — an agriculturist or an artisan, though the latter works physically, still has to think, but in this case the thinking cannot be compared with the thinking of a scientist in the atomic age. The importance of labor, in the progress of humanity, is emphasized not only by materialists but also by idealists, but with a difference. The materialists say that a person became a person only through labor and that the basic organ which changed the animal (the ape) into man was the hand. At the same time, they assert, labor with the hand constantly perfected the brain and this, put together, caused the tremendous progress of the animal. But this concept, which has remained only a hypothesis, can be easily met by the idealistic arguments which have more facts to sustain their theory.

In addition to this hypothesis, the materialists have developed others: the possibility of the transmutation of inorganic matter into organic, but no present facts sustain even this hypothesis. Let us consider the first question, i.e., the question of the perfecting of all the organs of an ape, including the brain, which came to such a high degree of perfection that after some long period the ape turned into a man. If this were so, we could not have the opportunity to see apes in the world today, for man would have taken the place of the ape. Yet, we see that, even today, apes exists which are very similar to men and they live the same life as apes did many thousands of years ago, but we can notice no improvement in their life. Even if science were able to show in fact that the ape and man in their first beginning had a common cell, even this far-reaching assumption does not lower the value of man, for it does not prove that man from a psychic point of view is identical with an ape.

The young cell has a rounded form. As it grows older, the form of the cell lengthens, and in the process it grows thicker at the ends and rounded, and the middle slowly narrows. Later there comes a moment when the two halves of the cell are connected only at one point, the so-called "point of contact", but this lasts a very short time for immediately afterwards a separation occurs. Hence, the first half of the primitive cell could have retained a soul of the second category, that is, a sensual (sensitive) soul, while the second half of the primitive cell at the moment of separation was judged worthy to become the possessor of a soul of the highest degree, that is, the reasoning (rational) soul which possesses the possibility of infinite progress. Thus, man, although in the Stone Age he lived an almost animal life and a life on the lowest grade of primitivism which lasted a very long time, still was able to progress and this, as we see from his inventions, is becoming infinite. On the other hand, the ape, although it lives along with man, has not shown the slightest progress and in the best case is only capable of mimicking what man does before its eyes.

The second question, the transition of inorganic matter into organic. For better comprehension, it is pointed out that there are three kinds of soul. That of the lowest degree is the vegetative soul which plants possess. Its characteristic feature is that it makes a plant capable of taking in the needed gases, drawing in minerals by its roots, and of a chemical process taking place in its leaves. The plant grows and is capable of bearing fruit, and this in turn enables the plant again to propagate itself, for fruit contains the principle of life imperceptible, which essentially separates organic substances from inorganic substances.

The second degree of the soul is the sensual soul which animals have. This has the qualities of the preceding, in addition to which it also contains instinct.

The highest degree of the soul is the reasoning soul, the mark of man. It has the qualities of the preceding two kinds of soul, and it also gives man the possibility of creating new concepts and of making his own judgments which the soul of the second degree cannot do. It is, therefore, impossible to think of the transition of inorganic matter into organic matter, for inorganic matter does not contain the principle of life, merely kinetic power; the principle of life is only possessed by organic nature.

Returning to the problem of labor, we must again emphasize that the influence of labor on the psyche of man depends first upon its content. There are tasks which have a bad influence on the character of a person as, for example, slave labor and similar occupations, for they kill initiative in a man. Yet, speaking in general of labor, we first ascribe to it the fact that it has taught man to think and also to speak. At the same time, its formative role is so great, as we see in practical life, that every industrious person is at the same time an exemplary person from every point of view.

### Overworking and Its Unhealthy Results

Every person knows from his own experience that he can work only to certain limits, and these cover a more or less extended amount of labor for every individual which depends on the physical or psychic strength of the given individual. Every person feels physically and psychically where his limit of work is, for then productivity falls, the result of the work becomes qualitatively worse and his discomfort finally fully convinces him that psychically and physically he has reached complete exhaustion. Great over-exertion even causes unusual disgust for and even aversion to work. This is a sign of the poisoning of the organism by toxins, i.e., products of decomposition which have greatly multiplied in the organism because of hard and uninterrupted work. The poisoning of the organism has a tremendous negative effect on the nervous system. Fatigue of this kind is called objective fatigue, for actually the entire organism is over-exerted and demands speedy physical rest as well as psychic release. Physical rest usually begins more rapidly and requires a shorter period. Psychic rest, however, does not begin at once and so must last longer, although physical work brings on fatigue more quickly than does intellectual work.

In addition to objective fatigue, there is also subjective fatigue which occurs when a person feels a great unwillingness to continue his work, and desires to leave it; this compulsion tends to exhaust him to such a degree that in the end all his strength disappears. There are also cases where a person is overtired physically but does not feel this exhaustion, because the activity in which he is engaged is in the sphere of his greatest interest.

There are also many other factors which cause fatigue. They can be of psychic nature or physical, and some can have their starting point outside, and others inside the person. But here we must stress that fatigue in the first place depends upon the content of the given work, for one or another work can be easier or harder.

The classification of work is very important in the arranging of teaching programs. Dry, difficult, theoretical subjects are recommended to be studied or taught in schools in the early hours of instruction, when the mind is still unwearied by other less difficult subjects, and the more practical, lighter subjects should be taught in the later hours. It is recommended that exercise be given in the last hour of instruction for it quickly tires the organism, which interferes with the teaching of other subjects for, because of physical fatigue, the attention of the student does not function properly. Often a subject may be uninteresting and difficult, but a proper and good method of teaching makes it acceptable and easily comprehensible, and after such an hour of instruction the pupils do not feel great fatigue.

Visual instruction is considered the most comprehensive for it is conducive to the understanding as well as assimilation of a given discipline by the students, while theoretically abstract instruction produces the opposite result. Modern pedagogy, therefore, strives to present theoretical and abstract instruction by visual methods as often as possible so that the understanding and learning of the material may, thereby, be more easily acquired and remain longer in the memory of the student.

Very often, the very appearance of the teacher wearies the students. We often find teachers who before they even begin the lecture on their discipline, by their official manner, the tone of their voice, their approach to the children, and their method, succeed in so alienating the students that even with the greatest good will the students are unable to understand properly and to remember the given discipline.

The productivity of work also in large part depends upon the conditions in which it takes place. First of all, both the teacher and the students must have a proper amount of fresh air, for good results cannot be expected from the work if the instruction takes place in a small room with the windows tightly closed. The lack of fresh air quickly wearies and much more rapidly than the work itself. The temperature also has an equally important bearing. Work at night is least productive. The seasons of the year also have a great influence upon the productivity of the work. Autumn is the most productive period. This season of year not only favors physical but also intellectual work. Spring is the least productive period of the year. A further contributing factor to fatigue is the age of a person. Surfeiting with food and hunger also influence productivity. Most productive and most advantageous to health is systematic work according to a definite plan. It is most productive and simultaneously endows a person with physical and psychic health. Industrious people live long and enjoy life to the end of their days.

### The Self-Development and Self-Education of the Student

The time has come to stop instruction which rests only on the assignment and explanation of homework and on its correction. Chief attention must be directed to independent work by students in school in the field of all intellectual subjects.

Biological experiments have shown that every living thing strives to increase and strengthen its capacity for life, that pleasure and gratification increases it, and pain and annoyance reduce it. Involuntary, imposed tasks performed without any interest do not have a good influence on a child. The first and main task of every teacher and educator is to comprehend the soul of the child and to understand it; this will facilitate the work of the child and will arouse its creative interest. In other words, educators must seek the beginnings of their work in the child and not outside him. There are teachers who pay no attention to the children whom the program is to serve, but place all their stress on the program which the pupils must complete. If the teachers approach the work of instructon or education in this way, they can assume that the students will learn the material without the slightest interest in it and, therefore, the profit is not great. The teacher first must theoretically and factually convey the connection of definite information with the vital needs of the student. We cannot overlook this responsibility of the teacher, for otherwise his work will in no way differ from the system of instruction in the Middle Ages.

The student must assimilate some scholarly material, but this must be basic; he must not work for long periods of time outside of school, but he should apply himself methodically and intelligently. There will be much more profit if the school, instead of a heavy ballast, gives the student what is most necessary, what he will encounter most frequently in life. Extensive material is turned into abstract and dry material for it is usually overloaded with a great quantity of definitions. Practice has shown that the productivity of thought will be greater in ratio to its greater concentration around some central theme. There is no need to broaden immediately the scope of our activity for this only debases the temper and causes distraction. The mind which is overloaded with a great quantity of material cannot fully absorb it, for it is overloaded by a foreign method of thinking and alien judgments. The school must first be based upon psychology. It must always follow the path of the natural process of recognition, i.e., beginning from the need which a person feels to the eventual utilization of knowledge as the chief tool without which he cannot perform his task.

Furthermore, the school must take into account independent creativity, the good mood of the students, and good self-confidence which is customary in every person, and especially in a child. The school should not suddenly impose on the students a whole mountain of definitions with which the student does not know how to deal. The school is not very concerned that in life the pupil will not be able to adapt even one of these definitions for practical use, it merely exerts all its powers that the material be fully exhausted. The school must first accustom the pupils to struggle against obstacles in life so as to make them inured to life, but the main thing here is that they must know why they are struggling, why it is their duty to struggle against obstacles in the course of life.

## The Interest of the Students

The young people must learn to overcome various obstacles but this must be done out of an intense interest in a chosen goal. Psychology states that the human mind works constantly and that this is a process in which the various parts of the mind examine phenomena in turn; then we observe, we imagine, we assert, and we create. It is not good to focus attention on only one activity, for in a short time this activity becomes boring to us. In the same manner, one-sided teaching also bores, for the mind then works in only one and the same direction. At the same time, the teachers must not consider boredom as being laziness. It is only a loss of psychic energy, which is a completely natural fact, that cannot be removed either by compulsion or by the fear of punishment. Rather, the teacher should instruct in such a manner that the mind could work simultaneously in various ways, so that the student would not only remember but would also try to investigate, so that they could translate their newly acquired knowledge into activity. This will arouse their interest and then the teacher will no longer observe discouragement or even fatigue.

The school must not treat instruction and education superficially. The passive acceptance of knowledge, as well as the constant, senseless sitting in school not only damage the physical make up of the child but also cause an equally harmful psychic damage. The new system of instruction brought the so-called "freedom of method" into the school, i.e., that the new programs of instruction of all subjects leave to the teacher full freedom in his choice of method; however, the basic principles of didactics are clearly emphasized as are those of methodology. At the same time, the new programs remind the teacher of the danger of any one exclusive method which might embrace the whole of knowledge. The teachers must at all costs in practice apply a variety of methodological devices which quite naturally appear in the process of instruction.

The new system in teaching emphasizes that in the teaching of all scholarly subjects it is necessary always to direct the attention of the child to the problems of a man and to his social interests. Also, the science of every subject must be connected with the teaching about man as well as about society. Utilitarianism, while it must not be allowed to dominate without any competition in all the processes of instruction and education, must be accorded its natural place in the problems of the school.[1]

1. *Shlyakh Navchannya ta Vykhovannya.* Lviv, October-November-December, 1933.

The school is unable to give the child a well-rounded and full knowledge, but it must awaken in every single student his independent drive to learn and must also offer the method for this learning. If the teachers wish to acquaint the children with all of universal history, they must do so very superficially, but if they wish to give to the children an esthetic taste and an independent critical judgment, they must take only the most important authors and they must then analyze all their works very carefully.

The old classical gymnasium demanded industriousness from the students perhaps sometimes in an over-detailed and too strong fashion, but this industriousness had its direction and its goal with perhaps somewhat excessive labor. However, the later gymnasia of the so-called "new-type" and American high schools greatly deviated from the old type and consequently have these results: the graduate of today has no real knowledge of literature, history, or mathematics. It often is said of education in elementary or secondary schools, the program designates the hour only for instruction but it assigns no time to education. One must not forget that instruction is closely connected with education. Education also depends upon the program of instruction and the quality and quantity of the subjects of instruction.

Once and for all, the school must stop believing that it can so arrange the program of instruction that it will simultaneously teach and educate, and refuse to assign a definite time for education. In such a case, the teachers can foresee that all the efforts exerted by the school to raise the moral quality of the youth will be ineffective. There is really no time assigned for education in the school because, if the school program of instruction takes education into consideration, it is very superficial and does not allot definite time for it. The program is so arranged that not only does the student have insufficient time, but sufficient time is also lacking for the teacher.

Very often it can be noticed that the class preceptor does not have enough time to become sufficiently acquainted with his charges, for much of his time is taken up with meetings and conferences which very often are not well planned, and the profit from them is, therefore, minimal, except, perhaps, for the increase in the number of minutes recorded in the books.

All the teachers must occupy themselves with education and on all occasions, in various circumstances, and even during instruction periods the teacher can insert his observations which pertain to education. In addition to the efforts of the teachers, the school organizations, which are regarded in the secondary schools as subsidiary educational institutions, must also occupy themselves with education, unless they are merely connected with the school, i.e., that the school program does not allot them a definite time. For work in these organizations a special time must be assigned; otherwise, it will collide with instruction time in the school.

The modern system of instruction and education is based on the teacher working out a certain part of the program of instruction along with the students, his giving the students a method of independent work and making efforts to arouse an interest in the students in this work. Thus, the student, on finishing the school, is ready for life, for not only his mind but also his character will have reached the level of maturity. The education of the student must not end with the completion of school. The student must continue working independently and voluntarily, but he must have obtained the basis for and the method of this further self-education during his study in the school.

Self-education is the only guarantee for a good future for every person. But the problem of self-education places before us a whole series of obstacles. The educator must, therefore, indicate to the students the way approximately to achieve their goal. The teacher primarily must awaken in the students a strong faith in the possibility of fulfilling all previously noted plans through self-education. Otherwise, the students will see in self-education a series of bitter and hard obligations which will be chains on the paths of their lives, and they will not understand that the goal of life in actuality is the increasing of intellectual and moral values.

## MORALS AS THE BASIS OF EDUCATION

*Morals at the Present Time*

Everyone of us certainly must not allow morals to suffer, because of the lack of boldness and through indifference. The present time is a time of great international struggle in military technique. We must, at all costs, revive the idea of morality which wars and difficult times have forced into obscurity and have, instead, placed the breaking of the atom in the first place. Today, only morality is able to shape a new man who can alter the standard by which modern youth is taught and educated.

We need man to be of strong character, of full devotion, and of dedication to the good of others. The revival of morality is a greater accomplishment than the most powerful military invention, for it regenerates all humanity and clears up minds corrupted by rivalry and egotism. It helps to solve not only family problems but also the most complicated political problems which exist everywhere on our earth. Morality forms a clearly defined basis for mutual relations and an approach to all problems, even those which might arise in the future. The power of morality is so great, because it is based on reason and the heart of man. Hence, by following the guidance of morality, one is on the direct path toward full and joyful victory. Each of us feels, in his mind or in his heart, that he has the seed of morality, for he reacts to inhuman demands. Only the animal instinct, which in some has grown to very great proportions, does not permit the seed of morality to germinate. The thirst for increasing his wealth, even at the cost of the happiness of others and even of life, too often pursues modern man.

The Twentieth Century, the period of great inventions in the field of technology and even of medicine, does not console us. Too many are convinced that these inventions will not bring happiness, for they are like a wild goat which has become separated from its flock and dashes wildly ahead to be the first to reach fertile pastures not realizing that it is easier for a huntsman to kill him when he is separated from the rest of the flock.

Today, as we stand face-to-face with our heightened, difficult problems of life, we cannot separate morality and look at it as something outmoded, secondary, and beneath our concern, for only a person who is very shortsighted in his calculations can be of this opinion. The wise commander, who seeks to defeat his enemy, sends a scout into the enemy camp with the mission of checking reports and getting information about everything, but especially about the morale of the hostile army. Morale is that power which can be applied even with very primitive weapons, and it will produce an inconceivably good result. It seems strange, therefore, when it is noticed that the leaders of the state often care for everything, protect everything by proper laws, but almost neglect the kernel of morality which exists in the reason and the heart of man. The trend of civilization must indicate the way to morality, otherwise, man may leave the main road, or even perish.

## The Sources of Morality

Morality appears in those thoughts and conclusions which the individual teacher and the school try to implant in students, after they try to root out, as a wild weed, other ideas which do not fit into the program of instruction and education. One can see manifestations of morality in the present sports and the social life of the school. Morality is strongly demonstrated also in the definitions which scholars create and pupils learn. But, looking well for the source of morality and trying to find its original source, it is easy to see that morality has its beginnings in the Department of Education, in the methods and orders which are considered most correct, for they come from the most objective thinkers who have acquired competent experience by years of practice. The sources of morality are found also in the social sciences, in those problems which are discussed a great deal. They are found in literature — in novels, poems, and dramas which are taught in the schools, for they are considered good and profitable, because their importance lies in their variety of forms and styles. The sources of morality are also found in school organizations and in the celebration of both religious and national festivals.

They can be also seen in the framework of the chief school or teachers' assemblies and in lectures which are given by political leaders to children, but the best sources of morality are in the expositions of the teachers as well as in their private lives.

At the same time, morality automatically is everywhere and marks everywhere the decisions which have been and are being made by an organization or a higher institution. All decisions relate to the course of events which influence the conduct and relations of the youth. Thus, all judgments, as to the value of life, inevitably pass through and enter into the whole process of preparations and guidance through experience. Many teachers, during their work, have recognized the scheme of the structure of their subjects of teaching and many teachers say that the result of their moral teaching or of the moral coloring of some subjects can be seen very soon in the conduct of the students. A great responsibility falls on those who strive to use venom with the planned purpose of poisoning contemporary and future humanity.

## Moral Education

Morality is the very essence of education. The whole purpose of teaching is intertwined with it like a golden thread and, here and there, it easily can be discerned. It is not easy to define morality in a definite form; yet it can be said that morality is a conscious controlling of emotion and habits. One must approach life on all sides, realizing that doing this creates enthusiasm, the power of which can be directed into all our most fruitful endeavors. Every institution must take part in this effort. Beside the school, this task requires a reformed theatre and proper censorship of television programs, films, and children's magazines and published books. The churches also must show greater activity in the revival of morality. In considering the question, we come to the conclusion that we need a synthesis of all institutions which would have the mission of reviving the morality of all humanity; society must understand that the problem of morality is the most important of all problems, for it creates in the young the capacity to live and makes life pleasant and valuable.

Morality must be implanted in children from their earliest years, from the time when children begin to understand that they must obey the commands of their parents, commands which perhaps have to do with the cleanliness of the body, sleeping, or eating. Even at the earliest age, the resistance of children must be over-

come by a reasonable and intelligent method. First, there must
be embodied theoretically the ideas of morality in the mind of
the children. In the family and in the school, children must be
strengthened by examples taken from life in the main principles
which control and regulate humanity: religiousness, justice, truth-
fulness, moderation, industriousness, economy, and benevolence.

In general, four methods are practiced by which morality is
transplanted to youth from parents and the schools. Three of these
are direct, and one is indirect. The indirect method is related to the
parents who, by their exemplary lives and observations, must help
the school to train their children morally.

The second method is related to oral instruction in school. It is
based on various examples and on the life of the teacher. The third
method is related to a complete practical philosophy in the entire
school system. The fourth method is related to literature, reports,
and discussion. The material for reports is taken from history,
biography, and domestic life. Themes are employed which concern
the role of pleasures and sports.

Morality is naturally the most difficult problem, for consider
the great differences in views of people who discuss the theme of
moral education. Some say that morality is nothing but the
regulation of social contacts or a code of external laws for a
properly correct life. Generally, morality is considered a single
authority marking the road to one's ideals, which is also the road
to a new world and new concepts of life. It guides us, adds power
to create a proper life. This proper life is not defined mechanically,
but it arises out of the sources of moral freedom. The environment
and external influences can only assist life, but they do not furnish
a definite, stimulating force.

Moral education, in the usual sense of the word, indicates
instruction on the theme of morality. Such instruction can never
rest on coercion, for this does more harm than good. This kind
of instruction cannot be a dry and arbitrary statement, for it only
tires the students, and moral context bores them. Moral education
lies in the ability to make the student realistically capable of
approaching life — as realistically as the natural disposition of
the student permits. This naturally moral approach to life, in a
way, creates a new world, and the student must learn to understand it not as a whim which demands obedience and self-conse-
cration but as that which marks his life and makes him happy.

To achieve this higher aim, instruction and education must work together, for studies are linked closely with the life and conduct of a man, and with these the influence of morality must go hand-in-hand.

Of the disciplines of instruction, history lends itself well to the process of education. Here, the teacher must emphasize that the life of a man always goes smoothly if it is based on the principles of morality. This direction in teaching and education must be supported by definite cases from history or by facts from our own lives.

Centuries of experience have shown that moral training must be connected with religion, especially in teaching youth in elementary and secondary schools. In these schools, the power of religion in moral training is irreplaceable. In the higher classes of secondary schools there must be a somewhat different approach of the teacher to the pupils. The teacher must direct his lectures on a higher level and connect the unanimity of religion with the latest results of science, otherwise, the teaching of religion will have a negative, rather than a positive, result.

Moral principles must be approached also from philosophical grounds, so that the lecture may acquire a progressive freshness and not a dry compulsion.

Taking into consideration the great tasks of the pupils in the future, moral education must not be less important than the teaching of any other subject. Efforts should be made to introduce morality into life, into practical use not only in the school but everywhere. This can be accomplished most skillfully in an indirect manner. In order that the teaching of morality in the school be not lost, one must make every effort that the home, in which the pupil is being reared, is saturated with it, otherwise, the teaching of morality in the school will have little success. The student must be reminded constantly of his future, good, and happy life of which his moral progress is his prime safeguard as it is realized from today onward. Teaching by this method will lead the student naturally to love everything good and honorable and to abhor everything that is opposed to it. On the parent, school, and church rest largely the responsibility for the moral lives of their children, because the home, school, and church are institutions which have the direct possibility of influencing the spiritual development of the young people and have a large supply or arguments to substantiate the truth and purpose of their teaching of morality.

Society must also have in mind that which moral youth will be, in a short time, a moral society. With a moral society, we will not be building houses of correction and prisons for adolescents, but for the same money the society will build schools and libraries.

Every system of state government has its own educational ideal which is the basis and, simultaneously, the guide for the instructional and educational processes. The trends in the different countries, beginning with ancient times, have their own specific character. Here, we will not discuss the trends of education in different, individual countries nor differences between them. However, we will examine certain features of education which a truly moral person must have, in other words, a properly educated person who can live under every system of government, for he is far above acting against the laws of God and humanity.

Principally, the morality of a person cannot be artificial. He cannot pretend to be moral, because he fears that he might be punished with prison or with a fine. At the same time, he cannot claim to be moral only because he lives in a moral environment, which threatens to rid itself of immoral individuals. Yet, if conditions changed, there would not be a trace of morals in the given individual. First, the morality of a person must rest upon his free will, and his free will must be regulated by the character of his person.

Character, we must understand, first of all, to be those most elevated qualities of the soul of man which are the result of the efforts of his parents, the church, the school, and the environment, but are chiefly the result of his conscious work on himself. Not all children are born equally good or evil. Each of them has distinct natural qualities, a different temperament, and a different education. But a person who is aware that his natural qualities are in some way inferior to the qualities of other people will make every effort to be like the others in his conduct and not attract attention by his irregular inclinations. Eventually, this systematic work on himself also changes his temperament to a great extent, gives him the possibility of agreeing better with others, and also inspires other positive qualities which are requisite in a good person. In this case, social surroundings play a large role. A person can accept positively the influences of his environment or can reject them. But in the majority of cases, not only a child but an older person as well takes on the color of his social environment. He assimilates the views of his environment, the customs, and everything else. There are cases where a person of firm character, with his own view on life or any other question, tries to oppose the views of the community.

To say that a person is without character is a very radical judgment. Every person has a character, but the good features of his character may not equal the number of good qualities of another person. The fault does not fall entirely upon a person. The unfavorable features of his character, in the greatest part, are to be blamed first on parents, then the school and environment in which he grows up and is educated from his earliest childhood. The easiest way to learn whether a person has a good character is to determine whether he respects the opinion of others and actively participates in all activities and manifestations. The educated person tries to assimilate correct views and rests his efforts on positive, clear principles and bases.

Very often we hear people say that a certain person is good and must have been born good. It is undeniable that he could be born with a different, more or less tranquil temperament and with a larger or smaller number of talents, but his character is not given to him, for character is the result of his work on himself which sometimes takes place against the background of his bad natural inclinations, and not a suitable good environment. Thus, the character of a person is dependent greatly upon his free will. If a person has a bad character, this is a sign that he has not used all the possibilities which were within the scope of his free will. But the character is not something unchangeable, although it may seem so. We have many proofs in history that the character of very famous, historical figures changed beyond recognition. In these cases, there was involved many, different causes.

In analyzing the various philosophical concepts which concern the freedom of the will, it can be said in general that freedom of the will is the greatest privilege of a man, but it does not exist in the absolute sense of the word but only in a relative sense. Therefore, the freedom of an individual must not be limited by slavish rules, for it is already limited by its own nature. It is limited first by all the defects of the human body, its psychic features, and by circumstances. But the natural level of the limitation of the will of a person is not uniform. An individual of persistent character through determined work can remove very many obstacles from the course of his own life. On the other hand, persons with a weak character often give up their life struggle when they see an obstacle before them they cannot avoid.

Further marks of a man with character are a classifications of his endeavors. But the backbone of all his inclinations is his main endeavor which reveals the actual character of the person, and upon which depends the direction of the life and all the efforts of a person of character. At the same time, he tries to subdue all his other side trends to the main goal. Usually, this main trend in a person of character has its beginning in the idea of harmony, both in the narrow and the broad sense of the word. Furthermore, this trend becomes a mean in the life of the person, for he does not wish to injure the interests either of any individual or of society. If it is a question of purely personal profit, an individual of character very often gives up his own personal interests for the advantage of society, for he knows that work for the benefit of society makes his life more meaningful, but work only for his own personal interests lowers him spiritually and erases all the higher qualities of his humanity.

In the process of the formation of character, a very important role is played by the processes of the will, for they are connected with the processes of the mind. They create a certain outlook, in an individual, which has a great influence not only on the formation of his character but on his whole conduct, even on his most insignificant behavior. Therefore, relying on the historical factors and the criteria of reason, it can be concluded that true morality must be based upon the strong foundation of religion. Without religion, it is impossible to conceive of true morality, for, in the first degree religion elevates human dignity to the highest point. Religious morality does not recognize social classes but attempts to concentrate all men into a class of people who would live and work for the happiness of one another. Religion, in establishing the soul of a person in the prime position, sharply differentiates a human being from an animal and thus orders him to direct his actions to a higher goal. A person of principle, who is born and grows on a religious basis, is never guided by his temporary moods and desires, because he possesses deeply conscious and solid bases which include in their scope the good of society and its inviolability. A person of principles is a brave and manly person, and his courage is shown at every time and in every place. There are moments in the daily life of some persons when courage rises to inconceivable heroism, even to saving the life or the property of other weaker individuals.

Honor, in the most diverse forms, is one of these steadfast principles of a person. One can recognize an honorable man first by the fulfillment of all his obligations, for he values not only himself but also, in respecting the worth of another, he tries to keep his word and agreements. He does not abuse the property of society, his actions are direct, all lies and extortions are foreign to him and opposed to his nature. He clearly shows the features of altruism, solidarity and respect for others. He is restrained in all expressions and conduct, and this adds up to another quality, that of companionability.

A moral man is, first of all, a disciplined man, and his discipline is based on the criteria of reason and the awareness of his obligations. This quality of discipline appears as the center of his planning and organization. But discipline can be internal and external. The internal is conscious, for it rests on the awareness of obligations, i.e., on the criteria of our reason; the external is unconscious. In educating children, we must have in mind the first discipline, i.e., conscious discipline.

A disciplined person carefully outlines the plan of his daily activity, he does not overdo in work, for he understands that work beyond the norm will react unfavorably not only on his physical but also his psychic health. A disciplined person also knows how to make use of his leisure time; he certainly will spend it in the bosom of nature, in a close family or larger circle, but never in a dirty restaurant with a glass of liquor in company with unconscious drunkards. A disciplined person is a patient person, for he knows how to control himself and knows the limits of pleasure and of sorrow. He is optimistic or, at least, makes efforts to be such, for true optimism is very dependent upon the temperament of a person. In this case, however, we have in mind another optimism, that which stems from definite reasoning and solid bases, which a proper educational system deposits in the soul of a person in childhood. This kind of optimism is a mark of a truly reasoning and good person.

Besides these qualities, another quality of a moral person is determination. It is a quality particularly admired at the present time. Indecisive individuals, at the present time, are considered pessimistic persons. Times have passed when people lived in the lap of nature, took pleasure in it, and it did not press them. The modern times are different completely; they are times of an unceasing struggle for existence. The struggle can be won only by a person who has the quality of making a speedy decision, and those without it cannot keep step with life.

### The Formation of Personality

Various factors play an important role in forming a personality. The first, which probably has the greatest influence on a child, is the family in which the child lives and is brought up. In the family the most important role is played by the mother, but the mother can accomplish very little if the father is not aware of his own responsibilities. Before formal education commences, parents must realize that they bear a tremendous responsibility for the developing of the psychic and physical qualities of their child as well as for its future. At the same time, this clear responsibility must reconcile the father and mother on questions of the method of rearing and of protecting their children in the best manner of which they are capable. The parents must not forget that agreement of the parents in these questions greatly facilitates the educational process, and disagreement between father and mother frustrates this educational process.

Education is a very complicated thing, and it demands proper preparation. The teacher is expected to have adequate knowledge of psychology and educational method. Quite often the teacher carries out perfectly proper instruction by a given method which best fits the age of the children and the circumstances, but the result of the correct work of the teacher is scarcely noticeable on many children, and on some there is absolutely no progress to be seen either in knowledge or conduct. After a long review of the circumstances in which some children live, we came to the conclusion that all these gains which they make at school they tend to lose at home, because the parents apply another method with the children, and this differs entirely from that of the school system, in addition, disagreement between the parents totally destroys what has been accomplished at school. Therefore, frequent conferences between parents and school are necessary to give parents more-or-less a guide by which they must carry on the process of education at home.

Parents must realize that the family has an enormous influence on the education of the children. What sort of a family it is, it is clear at a glance from the children. Wise parents know that they must adopt definite times for feeding the children, that they must dress the children in good taste, and maintain national or ritualistic traditions, for these are our inheritance which must be transmitted to those who come after us. The parents must guard traditions, and then the children themselves will certainly value them. Even in their childhood, they will not only respect tradition, but, first of all, will regard their parents as people who are fully worthy of honor.

As soon as an infant grows into childhood, without long hesitation, he must be enrolled in a kindergarten. There he will learn to be interested in life and the phenomena of nature and will receive an answer to all his questions. Being together with other children, the child develops intellectually, and he also becomes social to a certain degree. He begins to demonstrate the features of solidarity, tact, organization and, especially, discipline.

After kindergarten, the first years of formal instruction begin in school. The school, in the modern system of instruction and education, cannot be only an instructional establishment to give the child knowledge. Society must reorganize the modern school so that it will not only give a larger amount of knowledge than it does now, but also so that the teachers will take on the obligation of educating. By not recognizing or by separating these responsibilities, we may cause the mutilation of the psyche of the child.

Moral education also includes the training of a healthy patriotism, love for one's country. This patriotism must be devoid of any chauvinism, which brings no good, only deforms a person, and makes him like a savage beast. Patriotism is healthy when it is founded on the principles of morality. So the school, which daily has the child within its walls for the longest period of time, must also take this obligation upon itself. Education first must show the elemental attachment of the child to nature, to his own customs, to his language, and to his people. In this elemental attachment, true patriotism takes its rise.

In the training in patriotism much help is given by national festivals, songs, and historical tales. We must not forget that in the process of play, the child finds his greatest pleasure; it then most quickly becomes attached to his friends, to nature, to his own village or town, and chiefly to his family. These all enter the soul of the child almost unconsciously and remain in his memory to the end of his life. Singing and playing have an enormous influence on the psyche of a child. The chief basis for training in patriotism is the development of an elemental love for the native country, which usually, in the first years of childhood, is based on instinct and custom. On this basis there is developed conscious patriotic love.

Love for various places — neighborhoods and, also, the native land — is based in childhood on deep psychological experiences. Childhood receives external impressions differently, and it accepts them without the slightest hesitation. Hence, love for the fatherland, in the beginning, must be based on love for the regional nature which the child feels deeply, and these experiences in childhood will remain to old age. But, after these charming, deep experiences, while at home, near their parents, and later in kindergarten, sad days often follow which for many people go on to the end of their lives without interruption. Sad days often begin in a child when he finishes his pleasures in the kindergarten and passes on to instruction in the school. This period is depicted in very definite colors by Prof. Hryhoriy Vashchenko.[1]

When the child crosses the threshold of the school, he enters a new world which differs in every form from his family, home and kindergarten. Here, there are fewer pleasures, less laughter, and less occasions for joy. He may not have a smiling kindergarten teacher. His teacher may be a nervous, disgusted teacher who, from the first day, tries to direct the life of the child into completely unhappy paths. Even at this moment, some contemporary schools show great lacks and abnormalities which appear either in the approach to the children or in the method of instruction of these young students. At this moment, the child, whether he wants to, or not, must give up his special efforts or his childish stunts, for the teacher brings his life under a well-worn stereotype. This destroys his love of learning and, also, even for his stay in school.

1. Vashchenko, Hryhoriy, *Vykhovannya Voli i Kharakteru*, Munich, Druckgenossenschaft "Cicero" G. m. b. H., 1959, Part II, p. 156.

The child finds nothing but companionship in the contemporary school. The students of the higher classes are interested in sports to excess and, therefore, their scholastic achievements are scarcely noticeable. In such classes, there can be no question of the need for education in patriotism, for the student looks with suspicion on all that the teacher proposes to him. In attempting to cultivate patriotic education in the schools, the teachers first must remove formalism from the schools, that soul-less stereotype, and instead, must pay more attention to the psychic qualities of the child and consider the interests of the individual students. A proper approach to the children will give them a desire to study and, generally, a desire to pursue a positive activity in the school. There are many means of making instruction more interesting and the approach to the children more in accord with the nature of the child. These means are carefully discussed herein. See: The Methodology of Instruction and Education.

In considering education, one must first give thought to honor and the possession of principles. These important qualities must be fostered in the children, beginning with the earliest years. At this early date, the teachers must show the children that children too have dignity and honor which teachers must preserve. This consciousness in the child begins when he starts to differentiate himself from other people or from objects. Later, he becomes conscious of his own experiences, begins to differentiate acts which took place in the past from those of the present.

The dignity of a man is, therefore, the chief quality on which honor and principles are based. A worthy man never will misuse community goods, not because he fears punishment but only because such misuse is opposed to his own virtue. An honorable man will never rob the state or any person, nor will he counterfeit checks, for his human dignity does not allow him to do so. An honorable man will never steal state secrets, for his human dignity will not allow him to do so. An honorable man will not take bribes and will not blacken another person, for his human dignity will not permit it.

When it comes to the training of human dignity, it can be trained not only theoretically but practically. Under practical training, the child has the living examples of the parents, teachers, and environment. All these, if they have the good will to train a child or adolescent into a man with true honor and character, must show true dignity in their conduct. They must create a truly moral atmosphere which would exclude not only the fact but also the assumption of immoral conduct. But for this atmosphere to exist, there is as a prerequisite, the demand which pedagogy places before the parents, teachers, and environment, that they all keep their given word and promises, that there be not the slightest trace of corruption in their conduct, and that they properly perform their duties to the community.

In the presence of a child, older people must weigh all that they are going to say, for every inconsiderate word which comes from the lips of older people makes its responsive mark on the soul of the child. Older people do not often take account of this. The elders have been accustomed to think that children, especially when very young, do not understand what their elders are talking about and are not even interested. This is an absolutely false idea. Only a person who does not know the psyche of the child can believe this. As a proof of this, take an example from family life where the parents, without paying attention to the children, cast aspersions on members of their family or neighbors, and some time later they are greatly embarrassed because the children have repeated everything to those people of whom their parents were talking.

In bringing up children, adults constantly must give examples of the great successes of worthy people which are due not only to their industry but also to their honorable conduct. Parents and teachers must not forget that all instructions and examples must be based on reasonable principles. But in teaching these principles to the children, teachers must avoid the tone of Xanthippe which could fully destroy the vitality of the children, for this manner of speaking does not help the process of education but, on the contrary, it hinders the good sides of the educational process and disillusions the children with the teacher and the school. Examples from life must be given quietly, calmly, and even in a somewhat lowered tone, for this manner of speaking arouses interest not only in children but even in older people. At the same time, teachers must not hurt children's feelings, use indelicate words, or epithets, for this method of education demoralizes children. The stay in such a school, where children are demoralized, differs little from the confinement of criminals in prison. It is time that teachers understood that the child in school should feel vivacious and optimistic. This is in the interest of every person in society, for it is a prerequisite of their physical, intellectual, and cultural progress.

Vivaciousness and optimism not only aid in the physical development of the individual but often destroy the seeds of illnesses which children very often inherit from their parents or catch through infection. Vivaciousness is not frivolity toward work. The vivacious person realizes very well that there are obstacles on the path of his life, but he believes strongly in his own powers, and having before his eyes a clearly defined goal, he strives for it. Speaking of optimism, we are thinking of those higher forms which come from the beauty of nature and art. Its source is harmonious family life and good relations with others. It makes life pleasant and long lasting and it reveals a person in all human aspects. But its chief source is physical health. Therefore, we must adhere to the laws of hygiene, for in childhood the joyfulness of a child is chiefly connected with his physical health.

In early childhood, one must pay attention to the quality of the amusements so that they do not become monotonous, for monotonous games have a bad effect on the psyche of the child; they depress the will of the child, and the child not only does not develop initiative, but loses it completely. Yet, to have an optimistic mood dominate in the family or school, it must first come from the optimism of the parents or teachers. The parents and teachers must find pleasure and satisfaction in their work, otherwise, the home and school are not harmonious institutions. In an optimistic atmosphere new creative inclinations constantly will be born in the pupils who will continually develop initiative and active possibilities in them.

In spreading an optimistic mood in the young, the teachers will not forget to leave room for discipline, without which they cannot conceive of instruction or education. It is needed not only in the army, in commerce or politics, but discipline also is needed in the life of every person. Discipline has good quality in that it organizes life and bases it on definite principles and foundations. Without discipline teachers cannot conceive of the honest and substantial fulfillment of obligations, for it is chiefly, thanks to this, that we see the great progress in modern civilization. The organization of the private life of an individual must also keep well-defined norms. Discipline must have its application not only during instruction but also during recreation, for recreation also must have its norms. In a word, the field of education in discipline is very broad. The teaching of discipline and organization to the children can be carried on during excursions, walks, etc. It also is good to organize school evening-parties, for these present an opportunity to teach how to behave properly in society and with friends. In all these events the presence of teachers is essential.

Because morality is closely connected with temperament, we might devote some effort to a closer examination of temperaments, so that the dependence of morality on temperaments may be made clear.

Temperament is the nature-given psychophysical qualities of a person which reveal and also characterize the strength of the reactions to external stimuli. These reactions can be varied in vehemence and in duration, for every person reacts differently to stimuli and, at the same time, the duration of these stimuli in every person is different. Every one takes an insult differently, reacts to it differently, and keeps it in his memory for differing periods. These qualities of a person are called his temperament.

Relying on collected data, it can be said, in general, that temperament reveals the psycho-emotional and even the physical qualities of a person as well as the quality of his will, which in cases of stimulation is revealed by his movements and impulses.

Hippocrates saw the cause of this difference in the preponderance of one fluid or another in a given organism of a person. He considered the most basic fluids in the organism of a person to be red blood (arterial), black blood (venous), the bile, and the phlegm. The predominance of red blood in a person's organism gives a sanguine temperament, of black — a melancholy one, of bile — a choleric one, while phlegm produces a phlegmatic temperament. In addition to this ancient theory, there are many others, but the most popular theory is that of Kretschmer. He again connects temperament with the structure of the body of a person. He distinguishes four definite structures of a person: asthenic, pyknic, athletic, and dysplastic. Each of these corresponds to a type of body structure. Leshaft connects the temperament with the structure of the vascular system. The difference in the structure depends on the breadth of the vascular tubes, for their walls can be thinner or thicker.

Thus there are four forms of blood vessel structure and four temperaments connected with these.

The force of reactions to stimuli depend upon three factors:

1. The glands of the internal sections,
2. The structure of the organism,
3. The activity of the nervous system.

In the characterization of the temperaments themselves, the authors in general agree. The sanguine temperament is marked by rapid but not deep reactions to stimuli. The impression quickly passes over his exterior consciousness, for the sanguine person is interested in everything, but is interested in nothing deeply or for long. Such, too, are his perceptions. From pleasure, he can easily pass to sorrow. Cheerful moods usually predominate in a sanguine person.

The choleric person has quick reactions, but they are also strong and deep. The reaction of the choleric person is of drastic form and does not pass quickly. He stubbornly pursues his defined goal and pays no attention to obstacles.

The melancholy person has slow but deep reactions. Although the impressions spread slowly through him, they last a long time. He has sad experiences. He is prejudiced against everybody.

The final temperament is the phlegmatic. This is characterized by slow as well as weak reactions. The phlegmatic man almost never leaves a position of equilibrium, and it is not easy to arouse him to any action. He does everything by plan. Phlegmatic people are very often stubborn and consistent in their work, and this brings them to fine results.

These definitions generally give the characteristics of pure temperaments. Yet, pure, unmixed temperaments occur very rarely. The majority of people have combined temperaments. Temperament is given to a person at birth, and it marks the stable features of his personality. But temperament also is subject to various changes.

## IDEALISM IN EDUCATION

*Education from the Idealistic Point of View*

Idealism looks at education as a means and not something that is an end in itself. Idealistic education tries to ensure the spiritual values which parents and society desire to see in their children. The chief aim of the idealistic system in philosophy is the strengthening of realization of the Absolute Idea in individuals, in society, and in nations. This includes the concept of one idealistic social order which must be clearly evidenced in the democratic system of government.

Materialism is rooted in matter and takes the universe as a basis from which it deduces its materialistic system. Idealism stands on an entirely different position. It takes reason as a base. The materialist does not see reason in the universe, for he believes that everything came into being thanks to the force of energy and everything wise in the universe became combined only by a happy chance. So reason is nothing but the result of a great development of the nervous system in animals of the highest grade. Materialists state that matter is real and thought is only collaboration.

The idealist, on the other hand, gives special significance to the mind and builds on this his idealistic system. He maintains that when a person falls ill, he first turns to the mind, experience, and the intelligence which finds its place in his personality, but he never turns to matter or energy. The mind dominates matter. Matter is something else, for reason always takes first place. Reason is something clear, and matter only manifests itself by its external form.

Let us now consider the state. Idealists look at the state as a social institution, the task of which is to protect and further the moral values of its citizens. Idealists regard man as a reasonable and moral being who is capable of progressively revealing himself in human society, and who respects the Absolute Idea and moral advances. Recognizing the relative side in all natural forces, idealists in their views of individuals try to follow unchanging moral laws and try to be in full harmony with them in conducting their administrations. Idealists look at the state as a joining of the rational desires of many people who try by collaboration to realize the greatest ethical good for all. Idealists say that not only economic and intellectual good but all the values of life must be included in this organic system, for, as the character of the individual improves, the state progresses on its way toward perfection. At the same time, it is the duty of the state to arouse by wise efforts all the powers of the citizens to harmonious cooperation.

The state divides human society into groups, classifying them according to their moral and material values, i.e., reasonable capabilities, esthetic, ethical and religious avowals. It must be emphasized that every system of instruction and education must take into account all these aspects, or it will be considered incomplete. The idealistic system takes the position that all these given values must be inviolable, most highly respected, and eternal. Therefore, the idealist in teaching and education gives special significance to the knowledge of art, morality, and religion. He considers these as exalted and most worthy of respect.

### The Idea and Its Importance

The key to every person is his thought. Fixed and definitive thought, the rudder in the life of every man, is the idea which has first been formed by reason and is later evident in the actions of the person. A person is able to change only his viewpoint, when through reason he forms another idea which will begin to control him.

The creative power of a person is a movable circle which expands from a small thing, to something larger and larger and so on to infinity. For this circle to develop from a small to a constantly larger one, there must be internal power which would set the first circle in motion. This internal power is called our will power. Will power is entirely dependent on our understanding of and respect for ourselves. Our respect for our own self can rest on various foundations: inheritance, scientific or military distinctions, on the basis of various achievements, of origin, or even of material goods. It is not important on what basis our respect for ourselves rests, but it is very important whether we are planning to build a valuable structure on some one of these foundations.

Respect for our own ego must show only our reason, and it

must show externally only in our characteristic inclinations as well as by our deeds, but never in our words. The chief task of teachers is to temper will power in children and to engender self-respect in them.

A more accurate definition of the word idea, as Plato understood it, is that idea is the archetype of all created things. It is something immortal, only its non-essential forms can stop existing, and the idea can no longer appear in that form, but its content still exists and is constantly reborn but in other forms and, thus, it has an uninterrupted existence. Such ideas as we have in our mind not only have internal validity but even natural energy, for whatever they are, they always try to embody themselves in an act, in an activity. Thus, the artist must embody his ideas in an artistic work, an inventor fashions his ideas into inventions, a politician or a philosopher embodies them in the order of the state or in political efforts, and so everyone models his work, having had it in his mind perhaps even for a long time as an existing idea. All our lives, whatever they may be, are formed by our ideas. We try to grow into definite forms which are concentrated in our thought, and these are our ideas. Our lives are only uninterrupted action which is produced according to a certain pattern or form. The quality of the result of our acts is entirely dependent upon two factors:

1. The clarity of the idea in our thought,
2. Our management.

The first condition for a good result from our work in the educational field is the proper formation of the ideas of this instruction or education. First, teachers must know what to teach others. They must know what the school must give to children, how to organize, how to arrange, etc. Previously formulated knowledge comprise our ideas. Conversely, the experience of the teacher and observation of the students will produce in the mind of the teacher always new and valuable ideas.

A person, and above all a teacher, without ideas is like a hard rock on which no grain is able to take root. In practice, an idea is always capable of accomplishment, but we must add our efforts before it takes shape properly. When it is a question of ideals, they increase the value of our lives, they place in us the awareness of quality by means of which we become more valuable. The values of our lives enter the sphere of our actions through the intimate urging of our egos, our ideals. Every choice in harmony with our ideal brings into our lives valuable elements and destroys the less valuable. Our ideals motivate: Why must we live and for what? They are the motor and active forces. In motivating the aim of our lives, they, thereby, awaken our slumbering talents to their full manifestation.

Summing up the importance of ideals, we see that they:

1. Introduce value into lives,
2. Regulate the life of a person,
3. Motivate life.

Without ideals, the life of a man would be rather like the existence of an animal.

## ESTHETIC EDUCATION

The problem of esthetic education has always been and is now extremely important, for it includes the culminating features of the pedagogical ideal. Esthetic education is the most important element in the development of the modern cultured person. It develops esthetic feeling for the world and includes all artistic forms and colors. Esthetic education is also the center from which come the planning of the thought and imagination of artists who see the world more clearly in its esthetic character, and this feeling breaks through to the surface in certain defined forms. The problem of esthetic education also is very important, because the development of human solidarity is a necessary condition of social life which can be observed everywhere; society is divided into religious, party, and class groups. If esthetic education cannot be the entire source from which must come a mutual understanding of one's self, yet it will still be to a certain degree the main factor uniting all people in a cultural whole. The task of esthetic education joins that of ethical education, for ethical education polishes a person and helps religious education, it makes a person able to accept mystical, unattainable, and mathematically unproved truths.

Esthetic education cannot rest exclusively on the natural inclinations of an individual; for a child well can acquire esthetic taste through good education. The case is entirely different with talent, which a person is not able to acquire fully. Only the person who has it from birth can broaden it to some extent. To evaluate esthetic education properly, one must understand its psychophysical act which produces an entire complex of psychic experiences. It is most correct to evaluate esthetic education not so much from the esthetic side as from the pedagogical. In addition, teachers must always be aware under what guidance it is undertaken. To properly carry on esthetic education, a highly qualified person must be assigned to this very important work. We cannot imagine that a person with little or perhaps unsuitable qualifications could succeed in bringing out undetermined esthetic inclinations and capabilities and direct them to better forms, and, especially, do so without compulsion.

The second principle is that, as a guide in esthetic education, a person must be appointed who, beside suitable qualifications, must have those qualities and inclinations which he aims to seek out and guide to appropriate goals in others.

### The First Steps in Esthetic Education

Many of us still remember well the cradle songs of our mothers or other persons which deeply entered our souls in the very beginning of our lives, and our deep psychic experiences from them probably will remain in our memory to the end of our lives. As children, seldom do we understand the words of those songs, but their melody we feel deeply in our souls, because it comes from the bosoms of persons in whom ·we have great confidence. The cradle song is a great instrument of education. Mothers should have a definite supply of cradle songs, and they will produce in small children love for their native melodies and open the way along which their patriotic education will follow.

A second, important element of esthetic education is the story. Everyone remembers those unforgettable evenings when someone of the  family told of events which were far from reality. These stories were the cause of complicated processes which took root and broadened, in all directions in our souls. Children love to hear tales, because they instinctively feel that the tales enrich them, a quality that is true especially of folk tales which acquaint children with the creativity of the people, their life and beliefs, and expand creative inclinations in the children.

It is true that not all stories positively influence a child. We must not tell children terrifying stories, for they can injure the psychic structure of the child. However, stories in which we all see the victory of good over evil in their theme are a very good educational tool. It is good to tell stories not only in the home but also outdoors. It is necessary to call the attention of the child to nature, thus, to awaken love for his native place.

Further instruments of esthetic education are games of various kinds. Not only children but almost everyone psychically and physically love games. The reasons for playing vary: they may be instinct or, perhaps, the need for relaxation, functional satisfaction, or even to release excessively stored psychical and physical forces. The games must be chosen according to the age of the person. Teachers must cultivate the child's love to play at all cost, for it is closely connected with art. It produces imagination in children and makes them industrious and vital persons. But we must not interfere with children at play or intrude upon them, for in this way we take away their desire for self-expression. Children feel deeply about games which they have thought up themselves. Play imposed from above exhausts them and brings no profit. Undeniably, teachers must watch over children during their play time, but they must do so imperceptibly. The basic method lies in guiding the play of children into a path which leads to a better physical, psychical, and intellectual development of each child.

Parents and teachers must teach the children various forms of play and thus make the playing more interesting. The value of various forms of playing can best be explained by the kindergarten teacher, for in the kindergarten the children constantly request a change in the forms of their playing for otherwise it becomes boring to them. Prof. Hryhoriy Vashchenko recommends the use of so-called construction games, for they develop creative expressions and arouse the imagination of the children.[1] Children very willingly will build steamboats, trains, planes, and everything else.

Dances are one form of art, and they develop grace in the movements of a person. It should be evident that we are not here speaking of those dances which evolved in the African jungle. Recitations also contribute a great deal to education in esthetics. They develop in children love for their literature and also further education in patriotism.

In addition to these devices of esthetic education, there is music. Although certain inborn capabilities must exist in the child, every child must try to study music. He may have inborn but latent talents, and we must, therefore, give them the possibility of being aroused.

Painting is also an important tool in esthetic education. In kindergartens, children must be allowed to paint. It not only

1. Vashchenko, Hryhoriy, *Osnovy Estetychnoho Vykhovannya*, Munich, "Avangard" publisher, 1957, p. 25.

develops the esthetic taste, but it even refines a person to a great degree.

The completing factor in esthetic education is the environment in which the child lives and is trained. It plays a dominant role in esthetic education. First, it teaches the individual to conduct himself properly in society, to be social as well as courteous. Very often the school is unable to implant courtesy in the child, but this is accomplished easily by the environment in which the child grows up and is educated.

## The School as the Basis of Esthetic Education

The school is the most authoritative in the question of esthetic education. As the greatest factor of social life which forms the new generations, the school itself, thereby, determines the future not only of individuals but even of great peoples. The strength of the school lies in the fact that the ideal center of every peda- gogical problem always is relative to the final goal of every pedagogical activity and to the formation of personality. The school directs all its activity to certain definitely defined goals, and meanwhile it adheres to previously planned forms guaranteed by the experience of life. The true pedagogical ideal is by nature active and at the same time is responsible, and this responsibility lies not only on the individual pedagogues but also on the whole school. At the same time, this pedagogical ideal must have a universal content, to which fully correspond the generally known categories of truth, good, and beauty. Esthetic education will then have its constant significance, when it rests upon these categories.

Here, we ourselves see what great attention must be laid upon the environment in which the child passes his life even from the earliest years, for the true influence of esthetic development will appear in all its power only when not only the school, but the family, society and the entire environment in which the child lives and is educated is inspired by a true esthetic spirit. A harmonious person is a personality in which there is a full develop- ment of all human powers, in which the individual has his own style. Thus, the chief task of the school is to develop such a harmonious person. Every one who stylizes a personality takes this harmonious development into account.

Speaking of the importance of environment in the process of

esthetic education, we mean not only the environment in which
the child lives and is educated in the pre-school period but also
the formal school and its atmosphere. The exterior circumstances,
amid which the children live, according to their quality, delineate
the same type of positive or negative features in children's souls
which after some time also are evident externally.

The school, by its very appearance, must attract the child.
Above all, it must be clean, decorated properly in the instruction
classrooms with appropriate pictures; there must also be live
flowers, for esthetic surroundings are primarily conducive to
promoting esthetic education. The child certainly will be aware
that he is being taught in a clean schoolroom and so will want
to come to school in clean clothes and clean shoes. Clean shoes
and clothes will remind the child that he is a cultured person.
Therefore, his conduct will be noble, which means the excluding
in conversation of uncensured words and abusive language. For
proof of this I cite an example which certainly every one of
us has had the opportunity to notice in children during weekdays,
Sundays, and holidays. Children on a working day act differently
than on a festive holiday. The reasons are that on a festive
holiday, they dress better and their costume tells them to behave
differently.

Besides music, declamations, painting, and singing, great esthetic
education is rendered by those artistic performances practiced in
schools, because the students here have the opportunity to arouse
their frequently innate capabilities in all ways. During school
performances, the students have the opportunity to distinguish
themselves by their declamations, songs, dances, and music. At
the same time, these appearances deeply implant patriotism in
them which could not be accomplished by oral instruction.

When instruction ends in the school and vacations begin, it
is necessary to send the children for at least a short time to a
scout or other young educational camp, so that they become
practically accustomed to the inconveniences of life. Camping
helps children to choose the most esthetic path in which all the
work of life can be directed.

Upon reaching adolescence, the child begins to gain a viewpoint
on something more serious, for he then bases his thoughts in
larger part on understanding the basic questions of existence and
beauty. During this period, the adolescent draws up his plans

for the future and, beguiled by uninterrupted dreams, attempts creative activity in the field of art. Therefore, in this period, esthetic education acquires an even greater importance. During this period, young people must be provided with good literature; they must be given the opportunity to view serious performances, museums, picture galleries, exhibitions, and to go on excursions, and, especially, they must have the opportunity to work independently. The adolescent must learn to enter into independent life with a certain already formulated point of view or views which involve a proper understanding of beauty.

In analyzing more deeply the educational ideal, it is clear that each child must be treated as being a distinct individual, and this truth must be understood not only by each pedagogue but also by each parent. The development of an esthetic sense in a cultured person is the chief condition of his harmonious development, and it forms a definite and distinct branch of a harmonization of the person.

In analyzing the importance of the mission of the school in the educational process, we come to the conviction that the school must always be joined with life, and from that life the school must draw sustenance for its pedagogical work. The essence of esthetic education is beauty, and it must go along with life and creativity. Because the hateful and cruel struggle for existence, for the preservation of one's own self which ruins the material as well as the moral capital, this struggle for existence, which so strongly confounds sensitivity with estheticism at every step, can only have a barely partial justification if it is the final means and if in this struggle every one of us sees a higher goal.

## Theoretical and Practical Studies of Art

The last, and perhaps a more practical means of esthetic education, is the theoretical and practical study of art. These studies are needed not only for professional artistic knowledge but also for the general development of a cultured person. Unfortunately, contemporary art has forgotten about its natural sources, it has passed into the tangle of intellectual theories, it has broken with life by the slogan "Art for art's sake." So it has ceased to draw living sap from a healthy root, for work can create new possibilities but only with the aid of ever new material.

The true basis of art must not only be the understanding of objects and aims for which it can most properly be used. Knowledge which comes from diverse human efforts has as its goal the perfecting of definite accomplishments and fitting them to life, so that our lives in this way may reach a higher level, that is, become easier and more pleasant.

All education, and especially esthetic education, must come out of life; it must perfect all methods with the aid of which we might satisfy better the needs of life and eventually must turn back to life but only with the object of changing it for the better. Therefore, the study of art is an elemental need, for it develops esthetic taste as well as love for one or another branch of art. Furthermore, an interest in an artistic activity develops an esthetic universality which in this artistic activity embodies the most joyful and free activity, but with the condition that these studies are not compulsory. Plato proposed the education of children not by compulsion but by imparting knowledge to them through recreation, for the teachers have thus a better opportunity to determine their natural inclinations.

Again, in Spencer, of all the changes in educational principles, the greatest importance was laid upon the constant effort of parents and pedagogues to make the acquisition of knowledge as pleasant as possible for the children.

Esthetic education has as its main task the making of the assimilation of knowledge pleasant for children, not difficult or even unpleasant. Weber draws a detailed analogy between artistic creativity and pedagogical activity. For this, he chose as his basis, studies in the esthetic norm by Professor J. Folkesch in which the professor admits that the activity of a pedagogue cannot be subject to all the norms to which every free art is subject: the pedagogue in his relation to the child must derive everything from the so-called esthetic norm, which is called *Welt des Schönes.*[1]

During instruction and training, the attention of the pedagogue must be divided at least into two parts, that is, into attention turned upon himself and attention turned upon the students, and only then can his work have some esthetic value. It is important that he, the pedagogue, turn his attention upon himself, otherwise,

1. Weber, Karl J., *AEsthetik als pädagogische Grundwissenschaft,* Berlin, Wiegandt und Grieben, 1852, bl. 38.

fantasy can creep in which in time the children might accept as truth. Thus, they will understand a subject incorrectly. The teacher must turn his attention to individual children as well as to the whole group, so that he can better judge the finest approach by which they may grasp a given concept without great difficulty. The pedagogue, as an artist, must first orient himself on the extent of the psychic world of his children, for he cannot go in his teaching outside the limits of that world. The real pedagogue tries to choose appropriate educational material which at a given time would correspond to the children's psyche.

In every pedagogical act, the concept is marked by a plan, and the pedagogue must work according to that plan both in teaching and training. Esthetic education depends upon plans which accurately define the subject by means of which the teacher is able to guide it and which also suggest other means aiding the teacher in implementing his task.

Again Weber says, "The pedagogue must recognize the child's soul as an artist does nature, i.e., not by reason but by feelings."[1] Here, again, the question rises of pedagogical calling, which was discussed elsewhere.

Estheticism, in the full sense of the word, must emerge externally, directly from an esthetic center, i.e., from the esthetic soul of the given person. It must appear not only in his conscious and fully planned action but in all his movements, words, and even in his thought. And to realize this in actuality, training is required.

When it is again a question of the school, the method of instruction, and education, we remind ourselves of what unintelligent methods some of our teachers used, and they were supposed to be intelligent people. Certainly, not too many of us remember with pleasure our youthful years, that springtime of life which passes so quickly, and which we can only properly appreciate in our older years. That finest time, for many lives, was poisoned by inappropriate instruction and education in school. Formerly, too many schools were dominated by a rod or a stout stick, and even now such can be found. Montaigne in his time wanted to see flowers in a school and not a rod.[2]

1. Weber, Karl J., *AEsthetik als pädagogische Grundwissenschaft*, Berlin, Wiegandt und Grieben, 1852, bl. 174.
2. De Montaigne, Michel Eyquem, *Essais*, Paris, Librairie Garnier frères, 1948, vol. III.

## The Task of an Educator

It is the task of the educator to find suitable occasion to allow the appearance of the creative bent of children. They must first have freedom of choice of a goal and means, and this requires a kindly relation of the teacher to the students. Such kindliness in the teacher and the freedom connected with it are guarantees that each child will express his thoughts freely, and the characters of all children will be shown in their inclinations for creativity that not only seeks the best form, but, above all, that leads to their goal by the shortest route.

But freedom can lead students to laziness, and the teacher must not permit the students to remain in the confusion of their various, conflicting drives. It is the task of the teacher to find the innate natural inclinations and to guide them. The task of education is nothing else than the fostering of creative drive so that the obstacles may not cause unpleasantness to the individual but, to the contrary, that he might regard their conquest as a pleasant, personal sensation which every conqueror feels. Education must teach children to overcome obstacles, for in this way it trains them for voluntary, creative, and personal work. The work is not very fearful to them, and the nation which is composed of such individuals is transformed into a powerful national state.

The school also must feel that it has an obligation to teach students honorably to earn money by the most esthetic means; at the same time, students must know how to use their money in the most esthetic way. A person with many intended goals is unable to achieve them because of a lack of money, and this is a warning to children that they must acquire money in a suitable manner and use it intelligently. If teachers will educate children properly and well from their early youth, there will certainly be fewer of those estate bankruptcies which were prevalent before the war. There will not be so many excessive debts, fewer unpleasant scenes, and human endeavor will be more respected.

## ETHICAL EDUCATION

*Educational Ethics*

Ethics in education must rest upon the natural inclinations of an individual, that is, on his psychic disposition. It is the task of every educator first to recognize the inclinations in individuals. The teacher must endeavor, as soon as possible, to subdue bad inclinations, but he must not lose his equilibrium and, at the same time, must utilize the most natural means.

Under natural means, one must first understand a healthy and intelligent approach of the teacher toward the students. Children's natural inclinations must be given a proper outlet into the world. Teachers must carry on their educational work in such a manner that the good tendencies in the students could bring some profit to all students as well as to society in the future. In the opposite case, bad tendencies can gain control in an unexpected form, and then neither the best system of education nor the best teacher can direct the twisted soul of the young person into the right path.

In guiding the natural tendencies of students, the teacher simultaneously builds an urge in the students for self-education and improves the character of the students, while the activity of the teacher arouses their interest. Some children have such strong, bad tendencies that the teacher is unable to guide them in ways other than through the use of sports as the last resort in such a situation. Thus, in some cases, the school must utilize sports, excursions, and even (to some degree) amusements in schools, even if instruction might suffer to a certain degree. In such cases, control of children is very important. Society strongly must emphasize that at all student performances the presence of teachers is imperative, but the control of the students by the teachers must be imperceptible. In no case must the student realize that the teacher is controlling him, for this irritates the student. Then, the authority of the teacher drops in the eyes of the student, and he will see in the teacher none other than a police agent. The teacher will best be able to guide the pupil properly if the student regards him as his closest friend to whom he is willing to pour out his soul without hesitation. At the same time, no teacher should misuse the trust and sincerity of the student to scold him, but he must use it exclusively for the good of the student. In determining the natural inclinations of the students, the teacher will rouse a drive for self-development, which is the greatest aid in the educational process.

Education is creativity. While the teacher is educating, he is also creating, and it is exactly here that he must show his love for his students, for in them he best sees the results of his own hard work.

The first and chief aim of instruction and education is the properly good existence of an individual in all aspects. With this goal, there is a strong basis on which teachers can rest their teaching and educational activity. In principle, this means that the object of every person is first and foremost his own existence. Parents and teachers have a better possibility of arousing interest in children to ever-increasing limits of self-awareness in themselves when they produce in children the ambition to reveal themselves in their work.

But we must not understand this to mean that the teacher has to tolerate those bad inclinations which the child has inherited from his parents. We must first understand natural tendencies to mean those which induce the child to develop along one path and not another and which indicate the direction which leads to knowledge consonant with his nature. The teacher cannot tolerate evil, inherited inclinations. It is his firm duty to combat them, in a suitable way. If he is unsuccessful in his efforts, he must seek the advice of other pedagogues and psychologists.

In general, the most erudite pedagogues and psychologists maintain that not only the teacher but the father and mother as well can best recognize the natural tendencies of the child while he still lives in his natural and ordinary environment; however, the child constantly must be imperceptibly observed. If no proper natural environments exist, teachers must create them artificially, they must devise various situations which will seem natural to the child, for in such circumstances judgment as to inclinations will be more correct. The more diverse the circumstances, the more accurately the teacher can observe the student.

Turning to the question of the importance of awareness in education, and taking the position that consciousness is the basis of personality, education must deal the best that it can with consciousness, for otherwise we are not educating but training. Teachers are bound to take into account all the conditions of awareness which usually show the trend of each child's natural inclinations, for each person progresses by his own powers. But if we make such a demand, the demand for conscious action by a child, we must first allow the child freedom of thought and freedom for deep reflection.

Compulsion should not be applied in education. Modern education asserts that compulsion distorts the soul of young people, that it very often makes children shut themselves up within themselves, and then their natural inclinations turn in a completely opposite direction.

The teacher desiring to urge the students to conscious activity must make the children aware of the value of their activity. Self-understanding develops proportionally with increasing age. Therefore, as the child grows older, the teacher's encouragement toward definite actions should be stronger and should also be based on more rational examples. Teachers permit children the privilege of choosing their goal, for this increases faith in their own powers and increases their awareness of their own dignity. The teacher cannot forget that not only work assignments but amusements as well will fatigue children. He must give them freedom of choice, which will always rest on their inclinations. Sometimes, the teacher by his orders will quench the most joyful self-confidence. Then discernment fully disappears in the children, and work or even discernment and amusements assume the aspect of slavish fulfillment of obligations. We must always remember the words of Bacon: "Conquer Nature by Nature."

In the process of education, teachers must not undervalue the freedom of choice which is the highest personal right. Teachers will not get far if they compete against nature. Herbart says, "The direction of decision is an expression of character."[1]

When a school relies on compulsion, it very often warps the character of students, for freedom and activity are included in the expression of character. When it sets out a program of instruction, the school must arrange a place for free activity. In this case, teachers must find "the golden mean," i.e., they must arrange

1. Herbart, Johann F., *Allgemeine Pädagogik und Umriss pädagogischer Vorlesungen*, Leipzig, Siegismund & Volkening, 1876, bl. 152.

the program in such a manner that there is an appropriate area for self-educating activity. However, teachers must not resign their leadership in this self-educating activity. Here lies the greatest difficulty. They must so lead the student that every one of them feels and even is convinced that he is progressing himself, that no one is even paying attention to him.

### The Chief Task of the School

The first and chief task of the school is to inform the students of what will be most useful to them in their lives; the second is to prepare them for life. These are the two chief goals of instruction and education in schools. By preparation for life, must be understood the method by means of which the child will most successfully overcome all difficulties on the path of his life. The students must believe that their learning lies in their direct interest. So the school does not compel them to study, for they are studying not for the sake of the school but for their own life.

When we speak of a freedom of choice, this does not mean that the school is now to resign from discipline, without which it cannot realize either instruction nor education. At almost every step, the teacher must explain to the students why he gives directions, that he does so not to cause unpleasantness to the students, but that these directions and similar ones in the future will be advantageous not only to the student himself, but that society will profit as well.

In giving directions, the teacher himself must first view them seriously and strive to have the students fulfill them completely, else the teacher will lose his authority in the eyes of the students and this lack of respect will demoralize the students to a great degree. The teacher must live in sympathy with his students. He must rejoice together with them, and in case of a misfortune befalling one of the students, the teacher must show that he also is sharing his sorrow.

### The Dignity of the Student

Every person feels the need for self-respect. This need is inborn and lies in the soul of everyone, even the most contemptible person. Thus, in raising the dignity of the individual by obvious respect for him, we awake in that person the ambition which urges him to strive to ever better achievements. Therefore, the teacher must treat all the actions of students, even if they are ridiculous, with complete seriousness. Naturally, there must be a limit to such serious treatment, for by obvious pretense and artificial treatment, the teacher might impair the pupils' confidence in him. The teacher must not overstep "the golden mean," in his relations with his pupils, otherwise he will not be a pedagogue in the eyes of his students but will be considered artificial and unnatural. The attitude of the teachers must be serious. The serious teacher must not understand as a pattern, he must not inflate himself and act like a walking encyclopedia, but he must maintain a serious attitude toward his students in substance, for he must treat the young substantially.

The educator must become acquainted with the lives of his students to their slightest nuances. He must know the special ethos common to young people and even know the manner of speaking of his students, which is very little like the literary language. This does not mean that the teacher must cultivate all the customs of his students, but in beginning his work with the young he thus acquires a point of contact. The teacher always must try to remain young mentally, i.e., he must fully understand his pupils. He must understand the reason for their joy, sorrow, good and bad efforts. And by entering into the spirit of the matter, he must exert his own efforts paternally, as a true teacher and an intelligent person.

Herbart says that "the object of education is to teach the children to know how to live with people."[1] The teacher must translate this practically. He must try to live with his students as he lives with his equals. In this way, the students most quickly will absorb social ideals and will be self-confident always. In this case school cannot set detailed, accurately defined rules for the conduct of a teacher, for this depends on his personal intelligence and on his intuition. Every teacher must have good taste not only theoretically, but it must be part and parcel of the teacher, for, to teach others a way of life, he must first master the technique himself.

Teachers and parents must remember that children are gifted with a great capacity of observation, so that they cannot pretend

---

1. Herbart, Johann F., *Allgemeine Pädagogik und Umriss pädagogischer Vorlesungen*, Leipzig, Siegismund & Volkening, 1876, bl. 152.

before them. If we wish to demand something of others, we must first give the same of ourselves. We can easily recognize the value of a teacher by the very knowledge and training acquired by students. Often, a man who is gentlemanly and honorable, although not a pedagogue, can teach the children more than a person who has a whole store of pedagogical knowledge, but is essentially a man who is shallow and without backbone. The parents will be much wiser to entrust their children's education or even their boarding to the former people, i.e., to people with character and healthy thinking. A great wrong is done to children, their parents, and the people, when a government entrusts the education of the young generation chiefly to those who have appropriate qualifications, based only on diplomas. When the government fails to look into their lives and does not examine their course of life, the government may be guilty of approving some teachers who are of bad character.

A diploma is not enough for a teacher, seniority is not enough, for he must have qualities which make him higher than the average person and which make him worthy of being followed.

According to the psychology of Freud, example acts on the deeply implanted instinct of imitation, and even against the will of both the educator and the student. The example of the teacher unconsciously influences the child. Children turn their attention to it in various situations. At the same time, it acts on the students very delicately and imperceptibly.

The educator must have all those requisite qualities which are possessed by excellent leaders of groups or nations. The teacher not only must know the environment in which he acts, but he must embody the source of various concepts for inducement and organization. The thoughts of a teacher must be saturated with a moderate humor, for humor attracts the young, while a dry and formal mode of teaching repels them. But, for the example of the teacher to enter the soul of the young, he must be an authoritative person. His authority cannot rest only on the dignity of his office but also on his spiritual qualities.

In schools we must also develop organizational capacities in the students to a great degree, for today these are very necessary under all circumstances. Schools still exist today where no attention is paid to this aspect of the educational process. The chief reason why this is so and why some schools pay little thought to the development of the organizational capabilities of the young generation is that there is a deep chasm between psychology and life which causes this absence of activity. Psychology often makes no effort to see that its new advances find new application directly in life. Therefore, society loses the opportunity to utilize the influx of fresh questions of life, and life without the influx of healthy thinking follows the path of a well-worn pattern.

Ability to organize, to give orders, to see to their execution, the division of labor, and the responsibility which the organizer takes upon himself, the ability to make quick and definite decisions, are the chief qualities which a good organizer or leader has to possess.

The whole content of study and education in schools lies directly in teaching the young how to live. This is a very important question, it is fundamental, for in large degree it makes a person happy. The old sages made efforts to teach people this most important art. Unfortunately, at the present time when we are testing instruction and education in the schools, we can boldly assert that there is no science now which can teach people how to live. We can see the cause in the fact that science has begun more-and-more to remove itself from life, especially since most of its developments do not come from life and since certain of its advances are not necessary for life.

Theoretical studies are only subsidiary studies. The school must give students a theory of life. The teacher and the parents can transmit this theory in frequent conversations which can even be of a private nature. These private conversations can either be with individuals or with groups, i.e., with the children collectively. They can be in school or outside it, on all occasions and on different subjects, but chiefly on those themes which most interest the students. Such conversations of a private character refresh each child's mind which too often is overburdened with dry theory. At the same time, such conversations arouse in the young confidence in their teacher.

A further important means which strongly attaches the children to the teacher are private counsels, which the teacher gives the students on all their problems with which they turn to him. Private counsels and conversations awake ambition in the students as well as the desire for self-education. In private conversations, the teacher realizes his goal, because he can more concisely indicate to the students their ideal and the routes by which they can reach it without greater difficulties.

In this case, it is of prime importance that the school administration approve these private conversations, for otherwise teachers officially or unofficially will be divided into two camps, which will result in a moral disadvantage to the students.

In writing this, the author remembers one school where, among twelve teachers, there was one who acted as is described. He tried to live on friendly terms with the students and very frequently had private conversations with them, joined them in walks and even pastimes. Unfortunately, there was not a good result from his actions that there should have been. The activities of the teacher were considered both by the students and outsiders as very good, but the results were not in proportion to the labor expended. In analyzing the personality of this teacher and the method of his private conversations with the students, the author came to the firm conclusion that the chief reason for the insufficiently good result of his work was that his fellow-teachers held to the old, dry, and rigid patterns of teaching and education. They created such an atmosphere that the young modern teacher had no place for his pedagogical scope.

It is necessary that the entire teaching staff have one mind on the question of education. If this is not so, and there is not harmony among the teachers, it is useless to speak of a good result, for in no case will there be a profitable opportunity to influence children. The teachers' council does not have to create any special patterns, but freedom to influence the young must be agreed upon, otherwise, profitable work is impossible.

The teacher can influence the children by various means other than by conversations, advice, walks and pastimes; he also can influence them through such devices as praise, encouragement, and sometimes even by censures. Teachers must take care that praise is not so excessive as to demoralize the student. Praise should only confirm his higher status and must never lead to the student regarding himself as perfect. The chief object of praise is to encourage the child to better achievements. Praise must also compare the child's present status with the past. Furthermore, in censuring, the teacher must take care that the student does not lose confidence in his own powers, to correct his own mistakes.

When it is a question of corporal punishment, it can be said that it should be used in schools as rarely as possible, for in large degree it kills ambition in the student, and, in addition, the teachers as well as the parents, through using force, undermine their authority in the eyes of the children. The teacher must always have good relations with the children. When he has to punish a student, it is enough that he change the tone of his voice or add some cautioning word, and that is already punishment. It is in the interest of the teacher to treat the children as delicately as possible, for if a teacher talks for hours in a raised voice and one that is unpleasant, or even constantly scolds, that teacher has no resource left except to strike the children.

Teachers must not forget that the method of education of children is different from that which is used with older youth. When a teacher wishes to win his pupils through friendly conversations, he must, first of all, consider with whom he is talking, whether with pupils of the higher or of lower intelligence. It is not good to joke too often with students, for even if a joke has a good effect, this effect is very slight. A teacher does not win his students by joking, for his authority gradually will descend to the same level as that of his students. It is even less wise to joke with students of the lower grades, whose intellectual criteria are not yet properly developed.

If a teacher desires to produce a suitable fine result from his work, he must make his students aware of their goal, and, knowing this, the ambitious students will develop a strong will in themselves. Therefore, before a teacher begins to teach or educate, he must first indicate the goal and only then choose the method to accomplish it.

Primarily, the goal of education must be the attainment of higher ideals, but teachers must begin their progress by almost imperceptible actions. First they must teach children to handle seriously the most routine matters and, on this basis, they must direct the students to struggle for these higher ideals.

We have already mentioned that there is great educational importance in the school organizations. For the most part their error lies in the fact that in some schools there may be several organizations but they scarcely differ in their constitutions and especially in their activities outside the school, and so the student, although he belongs to all the organizations in the given school, has scarcely any more benefit than he would have by belonging only to one. The reason is that activities intrude upon each other in their spheres of action.

When it is a question of self-government in school organizations, it must embrace the youth of the entire school. In addition to the usual organizations in the school, there should also be purely ideological organizations which would be the backbone of the whole school.

A good influence on the education of the young is exerted also by boarding schools, but here we are not taking into consideration the so-called "barrack boarding schools" but only those where the children live the lives of intelligent families. An intelligent home in the field of education gives much more than a school.

When we consider the physical health of a child, we often hear the words of distinguished pedagogues who urge the transfer of elementary schools from the cities to the country. Such schools, however, would have to do more work with the students, so that their knowledge would not be sacrificed to physical health. In his university lectures, Prof. Hryhoriy Vashchenko often expressed this thought, for he believes that rural schools would be remedial institutions in the broader sense of the word. Their value would be reflected in the health of the children who could commute to them from large cities. An even better idea is that education could be transferred to the summer months, but with the condition that the elementary program would have to be modified correspondingly, both for the months in which the children study and also for the age of the students. In the coldest months, the children could remain at home with their parents, which would prevent a large number of illnesses.

A quite different picture is presented by the higher classes of the middle schools and the universities. These schools of necessity must be in large cities, in the greatest cultural centers, for the young people must make excursions which they could not make from the country. Another important reason why the young people of the higher classes of the middle schools or universities must be in the city, is that the city has libraries and museums. In a large city, the young people gain refinement in the broad sense of the word, for it is not only theoretical instruction that makes a person intelligent, but it is in greater part the intelligent environment in which he lives.

## CIVIC AND SOCIAL EDUCATION

*The Historical Development of Society*

The first man, after a very short time of existence in the world, realized the necessity of living in a community and not alone, for a community would help him to live a properly good existence.

Cooperation with other members of a community enabled him to cultivate the earth, taught him to make clothing, and also permitted him to leave his cave and live on the surface of the earth in huts built on the then primitive plan. So, day-by-day, his cooperation with others carved more-and-more clearly human features on the face of the first man.

When the first family was established, this brought about family life with a corresponding division of labor. The family began to progress through a common existence. In its life it began to differentiate itself more-and-more from the lives of animals. It discovered fire and, to keep the fire from going out, the woman constantly fed it with dry wood. The man went in search of food. So, in the very beginning, each of two primitive people felt that the existence of each of them alone would be very difficult. Of necessity these two primitive people began the first community which soon increased in number. With the advance of civilization, this community felt more strongly the necessity of a closer bond of all its members, partly to make life easier for themselves, partly to protect themselves from their enemies. Similarly, each family, even in its smallest form, was the basis of social unity, and it bound all its members most closely through its own interests.

With the growth of families, communities began to develop in the wider sense of the word. Several families built their homes on one small plot of ground and created the first settlements, which later became cities and states. But the knot which bound the community together was the common advantage, the common idea of achieving something better. Common efforts secure each member of the community. Thanks to community life, the lone man does not have to meet all the difficulties of life face-to-face.

Social structures can assume different forms, for they are dependent on the kind of life of the person and upon his efforts. In social structure there must also be included social law which is one of the most important factors that normalizes the relations of one member of the community to another and, at the same time, to the entire community. Simultaneously, each member of the community has a lawfully defined direction for his activity, and all these actions are directed to one common goal — the spiritual and physical good of the community.

With the intellectual development of individuals, their interests and inclinations began to differ which caused the members of the community to begin forming their own groups by which they hoped more rapidly to achieve their ideal. Each group had its tendencies which accurately defined the intellectual and psychic level of the members of the given group. The activities of the individual groups were often repeated, and such constant repetition of these actions led to deep-rooted habits. Such habits were shared not only by a few individuals but were also the shared habits of an entire community and were at the same time the reason why the community considered it necessary to create institutions. The very name "institution" denotes the common trend of the activity.

A very important institution in the community is the school, for it gives form to the community and at the same time strengthens it. The school by its activity initiates control over the community. The community is composed of individuals as well as groups which are joined by different forces of a social nature. These forces, at the same time, induce the community to activity in a given direction. They also are able to control the members of the community in three ways:

1. By the path of habit,
2. By the power of leadership,
3. By teaching methods.

Habits control society by pressure and by particular habitual processes of formulation which are peculiar to every community and cause its spiritual growth and very often even produce spontaneous reflex actions and undertakings. These primarily are tradition, customs, the spiritual aims of a given community, and all forms of art. In some societies, habits are so strong that they become a so-called traditional law, which no one dares to disregard. Thus, each on-coming generation is controlled by traditional laws.

The third means of controlling the community is the school. It appeared as a controlling factor in the very primitive community life of people, but not in the form which it has today. From the beginning of its existence, it occupied the most authoritative place in society. As we see, these three important factors are the product of the community and they serve its good. A man living alone could never attain a high level in the field of culture and civilization; therefore, the community is the source and means of progress.

## The Task of Civic and Social Education

The task of civic and social education is very important, for without it neither the individual nor society can achieve a better future. Analyzing the present time, which is also the forerunner of new future world occurrences, the task of the school must be to make the greatest efforts to assure that as much knowledge as possible is acquired by the whole of society. This would, thereby, find the best cultural method to solve all political and social problems. The task of pedagogy, in its relation to the entire society, is to adapt the whole nation for the future. However, the state and society must, first of all, create a suitable pedagogical atmosphere and physical conditions for the school to develop better its educational work on the young and, also, on the whole of society.

Besides school instruction and education, it is imperative that harmonious cooperation be maintained between children at school and their elders; this is true even in extra-mural activities. Thus, two streams will meet which will supplement each other and at the same time create one whole. The experience of the elders, their moderation and authority, will check the fires of youth. On the other hand, the energy of the youth, properly regulated by the elders, is able to break through all obstacles on the path of their own life and that of civic and state life. The older generation will set the youth on a suitable path which will not shake the faith of the youth in their own ability. Here, must be emphasized that the interference of older people with youth must have its boundaries, otherwise, it can provoke suspicion and disbelief and, later, also a disinclination to work.

To make the education of the young easier for teachers, the school can establish a school organization which would morally obligate the young to maintain, in their life outside school, all those principles which the school recommends. Under suitable leadership, such an organization can, like the school, develop discipline in the young and accustom them to work in the social field. An active member of a school organization usually becomes an active member of the community and the state.

The school organization is, at the same time, a field for the young to demonstrate their abilities, where they can awake their talents and increase their development. Whoever enters such an organization should not leave it until he becomes of age to enter immediately into an organization of young adults. Generally in no case should young people be permitted to leave one organization only to join another, for usually then, the work done by the first organization will have been wasted.

Young people in organizations must have as many meetings, councils, or sessions as reasonably possible, for this is a field in which they have the opportunity to fashion themselves and to prepare for their future social and political life. Discussions at such councils must be concrete and short. All disputes must be settled as rapidly as possible, decisions must not be put off, and it is the duty of the leadership to see that all resolutions are completely enacted. In school organizations, the young people will learn to submit to the general needs of society; but society's profit must not be allowed to be a bitter burden to the individual.

In every school, there must be reading rooms containing selected works on instruction and education. The teachers must also make reports in the school and outside it through which they could educate the youth and society in a community spirit.

When it is a question of civic and state education, in the broad sense of the word, each adult of the family must be a pedagogue who will see to it that he educates children in a civic and community spirit. In this spirit, every citizen of a state must be an educator.

The urge to achieve in individuals must rest on conscious, if not always immediate, then long-range service for the increase of our cultural treasures. However, we should not identify civic and social education with formal civic and social instruction, for then the best citizen of a state would be the one who has the most knowledge of political science.

Political intelligence is not education in a party, but it is even something opposed, for the party directly expresses the efforts of some social group under the pressure of certain interests, and the party represents a definite political concept which should grow out of definite needs of the people, from their aspirations and from the world situation with which they must get along. These factors enter into the program of the entire nation, and the nation must broaden its party awareness to the further limits, so as to understand all social questions; otherwise, it will not have a way out from unpleasant circumstances when confronting concrete situations. The first and chief task of a party is to understand the importance of its state. It must support all those actions which arouse the people to interest themselves in their state, in its cultural and political problems.

Analyzing civic and social education, it becomes clear that such education encompasses political education, for political education is possessed by every one who has secured a proper view of the goal of the state.

State and civic education must first of all be voluntary, for the moment that it tries to impose on all people of a given state identical social and moral obligations, it loses its brightness and ceases to be essentially itself.

On the basis of what has been said, the school must come to the final decision whether education is to teach individuals to produce something of service or whether individuals should be educated merely to slavishly follow other people's views. Knowing how to live is nothing else than knowing how to struggle, for eternal peace will dominate in the world only with the last man. The goal of civic and social education is to make war constantly more humane and peace constantly more voluntary. To be truly a citizen of a state means to serve a definite ideal, some supreme goal, but only the man with a properly formed character can do this.

The task of civic and social education is to create constantly new views resting on the firm basis of conviction and experience. It depends in large measure on the school that people might be able to have true and unwarped understanding, that the greatest actual concepts may have a broader and deeper comprehension by the people. It is necessary to educate people civically and socially not only in school but also outside of it, so that there may be a unity of thought in the nation. The teacher must serve the interests of the whole society. He must not occupy himself with any policy other than that which aims to unite all the citizens under the banner of his state. Teachers also must refrain from cultivating political views or movements which they believe will not redound in the future to the advantage of the society. The school must occupy a central position in the state, for it knows best how to find the "golden mean" where various views, various parties, and various races of the people in a given state can agree. Thus, the school must carry on education in the field of great questions and fashion in the citizens a point of view which suits the logical conclusions and the noble character of the majority of the citizens. The school must educate so that citizens would evolve with definite bases of opinion, supported by actual facts, but the school must first throw a true light on those facts.

The school is empowered to give the nation unwarped concepts, and these concepts must find complete and proper comprehension among the people. So, when we think of the civic and social education of the people, we must not forget that the most authoritative and decisive voice in the process of education is that of the school.

### Education in Two Directions

Under education in two main directions, we understand two main factors in education: the individual and society. Education is a process which makes constant changes in a person. The chief object of education is to teach an individual not to conform to certain unhealthy phases of his environment and at the same time to give him the strength by which he can influence his environment so that it too would submit to changed circumstances. Each individual first must take into account that he is a member of society and his special development, and even in large part his life, is dependent on the social side of his surroundings. The task of education is to adapt the individual to society, but it cannot permit this adaptation now or in the future to result in disadvantage to the individual. So the function of education is twofold:

1. The insuring of the development of the individual,
2. The individual must bring profit to society.

If we analyze the task of society, it will become clear that its chief objective is to bring profit to the individual. This activity of the school and education, in a broad sense, is a task which will never lose its importance, because it is solicitous for and, even to a great degree, it guarantees harmony in every society, without which it is impossible to visualize the prosperity and development of a nation. Proper education is not only the individualization of society, but it is also the socialization of the individual. The individualization of society makes its members useful and the socialization of the individual produces exemplary good members of the society as a whole. The subordination of the individual to the society is a stabilizing process which endeavors to maintain the order of old social institutions. A similar process of subordinating society to the commands of its leadership is, at the same time, an achievement of progress which daily enriches society in its special values.

Man, by his very nature, is a social animal. The law of individual life is also the law of social cooperation with a somewhat different application. Although a man is born a social animal, yet his egotistical instincts gain predominance. These instincts must be forced into a form which most ennobles the character of the given individual and which also compels him to renounce some of his own, obviously beneficial, personal possessions for the good of society. Living in society, the individual by the force of reality must perform certain communal obligations and, together with the other members, take part in the creation of spiritual and material values, defend his country, live a religious life, find solace in the community during the difficult moments of his life, and rejoice in the happiness, of others.

The law of the process of moralization is as strong equally for the individual and for the society. Furthermore, obedience to the community must be an essential balancing of the relation of the society toward every individual, for society, as well as every individual, possesses all the attributes of personality. The life of the community, as well as the life of the individual, is nothing but self-realization, self-development through its own discipline. Virtues, here, have their deepest application, for they are the basis on which rests the common life of the individual with society. If an individual, at least, in his views, supports the value of a high-quality society, this marks his emancipation from the limitations of individuals and, thereby, through his services to the community, he, so-to-speak, cuts a path through a dense forest toward self-realization.

The law of moral life and the law of personality cover the realm of both social and individual obligation. When evolution is traced, starting with its very beginnings, it is easy to come to the conviction that there is an organic relationship between the individual and the community. A man is not separated from mankind, for everything that he has comes from the community through transmittal or by inheritance. The individual is unable to separate himself from the community, because, as long as he lives, through his entire life, he will profit from the common goods of the entire community in one or another form. Society also as a whole is dependent to a definite degree upon every individual for every one of them contributes something of his own to the whole, to the common life. So society, in the broad sense of the word, is an organism which is composed of various kinds of members — each of whom fulfills his special and definite task.

The desires of the individual, family, and the community do not always go hand-in-hand. Very often, in certain definite aspects, there is a cleavage between them, either in views or even in their active fulfillment. Differences and misunderstandings in certain definite questions arise predominantly when a member of society has to resign for his own personal good for the benefit of society. An ambitious intelligent egoist automatically is reborn as an altruist, and this regeneration, resting on the natural law, is the strongest pledge for common life and mutual help. The individual first must be convinced that mutual effort guarantees a better future for his own self and that the common gain, in addition to being profitable, will also bring him moral satisfaction.

## The Government in Society

Order in society is protected by the government. Its task is not to permit a social catastrophe. It does its tasks by suppressing the harmful actions of individuals who threaten the good of the entire society. It also endeavors to facilitate the normal development of society by merging the progress of every individual. But the progress of the entire population is not only dependent on the government, but it is dependent above all, on individuals. Society only matures through work on itself, which work lies in cultivating social ties and increasing joint experience. The higher the society, the easier is the task of government, and so the more rewarding; along with this, the individual has the opportunity to enjoy greater freedom and laws, all of which taken together secure the long-lasting existence of a given state. Furthermore, the levels of society are better understood by each individual. Thus, the chief task of the government must be to reconcile the actions and rights of the individual with the rights and actions of the whole society and to bind them into one inseparable whole.

Today, not all individuals of society are able to understand the great advantages which are gained by social, harmonious living, which even insignificant creatures feel instinctively, when it is sometimes necessary for individuals to renounce their very insignificant personal goods in order to achieve together with society a material as well as moral profit. The reason for this stubbornness is nothing else but the fact that the mind of individuals is not far-sighted enough and does not, through logical conclusions, foresee the further results.

A healthy society is one that has deeply engraved in its soul the old and well-known words: *salus rei publicae — lex suprema est,* which mean that in that society reason has gained the upper hand over short-sighted primitive egotism. It is true that there is no sincere democracy where there are no strong ideological groupings which mingle their ideas with faith, but their victory must come from pure initiative, so that they can produce something new. Individuals, in such cases, can belong to groupings which hold views similar to their own, but they should not do so for purely personal interests or for the interests of the narrow circle holding the same views, but for the good of the entire society. Such groupings must not harm the common interests by overpowering each other, perhaps, even by inhuman methods, for then the authority of a democratic system and the good of the people will suffer. Then, the people will lose confidence in democratic principles and will seek a solution in totally opposed systems of state government.

The state in turn must guarantee a bilateral contract concluded between society and the individual, for in a state where the government is the main factor of union and individuals do not have full confidence in it, individuals are not able to enjoy that full freedom which gives them a greater desire to work for the good of society. In proportion to the growth of egotism, there grows, likewise, a lack of harmony in the whole society. And the entire social structure suffers, for it requires a great extension of the central machinery which devours great incomes from the efforts of the society and saddles it with a great burden.

## *The Scale of Living*

A very important social question concerns the scale of living of the members of the community. Every society is composed of individuals who have different material and moral values, and on these values chiefly depends their scale of living. If the living scale of all the individuals of a society is well calculated, the existing state order is approved officially or unofficially by every individual. So, it can be said that the chief obstacle in the creation of social communities is not perhaps the level of the founding capital, that is, the contribution of the peoples, but it, perhaps, is due more to lack of confidence.

The chief basis for confidence must be the conviction that a better developed people will not take advantage of the; fellow member and he, in turn, will not wish to enrich himself at the cost of another's work, but each by his own effort will try to reach a higher standard of living. Every one deserves the right to a better life and, at the same time, have the right to leadership in the community or the state. This, naturally, must be dependent upon the individual capabilities of every individual rather than on pointless, selfish reasons. This is a fully natural right, which no regime and no constitution dares to destroy. In this case, we must turn our attention to whether the existence of this right is emphasized directly by physical force or whether it is confirmed by a voluntary agreement, which is the result of the understanding of the aim and value of this right.

A suitable adjustment of the living scale is an extraordinarily constructive factor which guarantees, both to the individual and to whole nations, a healthy growth through the development of a noble-minded civilization.

## The Law of Freedom

Freedom is the most essential factor for the most correct development of the personality of individuals, and it is also indicative of the actual greatness of a nation. Freedom is the product of knowledge; the physical and intellectual development of all humanity is indebted to it. However, if such unfortunate situations would exist where science or politics would endeavor to destroy freedom, all of us certainly would say that such a science should vanish from the face of the earth, for it takes away freedom from those who created this very science. It is the sacred duty of every state leadership to protect the freedom of its citizens, increase and promulgate it. A true democratic state must exclude even the least signs of prejudice. There is no man on earth who has the right to place a yoke on the neck of another person, for every person who is born into the world enters the sphere of the law which secures it all human rights which no one dares to disregard.

The law of freedom is the sacred gift given to *every* person, and each person feels in his heart the right to possess it. It is almost an instinct essentially merged with our nature. No one has the right to disturb the freedom of a person for, in violating it, he violates the dignity of a man, a right which a man is entitled to defend.

When we speak of democratic freedom, in practice, an incorrect understanding of it is observed. Democratic freedom does not mean that every one who wants has the right to litter the streets or dump refuse in undesignated places. Democratic freedom does not mean that a student of the middle or even the elementary school has the right to smoke cigarettes in the presence of his teachers.

Democratic freedom also does not mean that children have the right to abuse their elders and heed no law, just because they are protected by the freedom of a democratic state. Democratic freedom means that every citizen has the right to do everything that brings him profit, or only brings him pleasure, but, at the same time, his activity must not harm others. If we tolerate unhygienic, unesthetic, or immoral efforts of degenerate individuals, we shall wrongly understand the freedom of democracy, then a democratic state will become a jungle.

### The School in a Democratic System of Government

A definition of democracy is: "Government by the people; a form of government in which the supreme power is retained by the people and exercised either directly or indirectly through a system of representation and delegated authority periodically renewed, as in a constitutional representative government, or republic." (Webster's Dictionary)

Here, having in mind the school in a democratic system of government, we can say that the entire life of an individual is, at the same time, its school, and that every individual is, at the same time, both a teacher and a student, and every relationship and event in life is in essence educational. We feel this ourselves without long consideration. Every mother, who teaches her children how to maintain order around them, is, at the same time, a teacher and assumes the responsibility for the education of her children. The mother, in this case, is a teacher to a high degree, and her responsibility before the government and the people is no less.

However, the responsibility of a teacher by profession becomes a great one. Now come the questions: What causes confidence in a teacher? What is the nature of this confidence? The nature of this confidence does not show forth in very definite colors or settings, but rather in secret and intimate ways. The nature of confidence lies in the great responsibility of the teacher to make great changes in society; they can be good or bad, useful to society, or the opposite.

The school stands in the middle of history. On one side is the past; and on the other the future. From the past, the school, whether it wants or not, must retain the scientific achievements of the different branches of learning, it appropriately must correlate these achievements with the achievements of the present and transmit culture to the future. The real questions are: How will it pass achievements to the future? How will it arrange them? What will it select and what will it reject? For after a certain time this will decide the aspect of a given society and what is to be its fate. We are not free whimsically to change the organization of the school, for this, without doubt, would call forth negative results, especially at the present time, when, in great parts of the world, the present generation is in great part passing from an agrarian to an industrial society.

The chief role of the teacher and the school in society is to teach every one, young and old, how to live and how to organize social, political, and economic institutions in all the circumstances which they may encounter. Thus, the central organization in the state is the school, for it sets the pattern for all the other institutions in society, it also defines the relations of the people to the state, to the church, and to their place of work, and these relations are based upon and are nourished by the accumulated knowledge which the school gives by its correct teachings.

Having in mind the ideology of education, the school must take the position that it must build instruction and education which would be based on truly democratic principles, for in a democratic system of government a person is a true person and has the opportunity fully to develop his personality. True democracy is the highest form of society, and this is progress.

At the same time, the people must not forget that a true democratic order is ruinous for a people who cannot rise to the level of noble-minded living in cooperation with others, for only a firm hand then will stop their personal calculations. A government can go hand-in-hand with the people and devote all its actions and powers to useful creativity only when society shows itself ripe for a cultural inner-living together.

A true democracy gives the opportunity to all its members to express themselves sincerely in proportion to their interest in that sphere where they show knowledge and interest. A democracy, among other things, will never lack leadership, for it always will secure wise leaders and a solid administration from within itself to which every citizen offers his obedience, for he has full confidence in it. Furthermore, each citizen of a democratic state must not busy himself exclusively with his calling without taking interest in social questions. For if he does, he negates the idea of democracy and exposes the people to the fate of chance.

If we look back at history, it is seen that all the great states had as their basis an idea on which their power was built. Such ideas were born in a large degree at the moment of the greatest decline of the population. For instance, when Rome (i.e. the Empire) was morally falling into an abyss, there was demoralizing in all corners of its empire. At that time, when religion was a matter of complete indifference and social thought had deteriorated, despots usurped the place of the old Roman democratic system. But salvation came for Rome, for on its moral ruins grew up a new idea — Christianity.

Christianity is the source of the broadest social and communal reforms. It rests on a spiritual basis. It is the idea of true social justice, for it is founded on moral principles, the goal of which is the union of all people in one flock, through a common idea of the social good. This idea secures social peace and a healthy and rapid progress for the better.

Democratic education must have definite concepts which mirror democracy. The ideal of democracy lies in the fact that the individual and society are mutually dependent on each other and mutually supplement each other. Democratic sanctions should never be used by the state as a means for taking advantage of an individual, nor should the individual hold the state in contempt. The goal of democratic education has as its task the organization of the community in such a manner so that every member has the opportunity to develop his personality through activity which profits not only himself but, also, all the other members of the community. The actual and correct ideal of democracy, the effective ideal, is permeated by cultural life which strives to produce a new person; not new in the sense that this person will know more and work more productively, but in the sense that he will have new relations toward the past, of which he is the fruit and will have new relations toward the future, from which he hopes to profit.

Thus, original power is produced in the nature of a person who draws his energy from new contacts with the world and mankind and who distributes his powers on all the paths of his life throughout his entire existence. Therefore, education in a democratic system must develop knowledge, interest, ideals, and tendencies in every individual, and every individual must be able to use all these for the good of all. In addition, the real goal of education is the training of children to be healthy, courageous and noble people. In this kind of education, we find four characteristics:

1. Exact observation,
2. Clear understanding,
3. Independent thinking,
4. The striving for continuous achievements.

All these are the objects which an effective ideal puts before us and which provide us with breadth in educational aspirations along the line of democracy; these take their beginning in the kindergartens and continue through the universities. This new means of instruction does not undervalue the accomplishments of the past centuries but takes those accomplishments into account while devising and practicing new methods.

The answers to the problems of democracy must come out of the schools, they must be born in the schools and also grow in the schools. Day and evening schools teach the young people accurately defined disciplines, yet the task is not satisfied by this. The task of the schools goes much further: the schools first must prepare every generation for life and must show the paths for improving democratic principles.

The democratic system must bring into the schools all the qualities and possibilities which would help in the development of democratic education, for the goal of democracy is the constant procurement of advantages and profits for the citizens of a democratic state.

Speaking of advantages, we must not be content only to gain material advantages with which old Rome was satiated, for these first caused Rome's decline. We must above all understand profits and advantages in the spiritual meaning of the word, i.e., that no one has the right to fetter our intellectual and spiritual powers by any means, for they are peculiar only to man and they have the power to reveal his personality at every step. Society must strive along this path to secure for every individual and every group all the possibilities of self-manifestation which are fully consonant with natural law on which the written law must be based. Only a state which treats every one in the same way, without distinction of nationality, race, color of skin, religion, the descent of the individual, or in what part of the world he was born, only a state providing such treatment of citizens will make them happy to a high degree and will see them accept the obligation to defend their democratic state.

## The Social Conscience

In the preceding sections of this work, we spoke of the renaissance of the school and with it of all mankind. But when we stop to consider this, we will come to the conviction that the problem of regeneration of a person is nothing but the problem of his conscience, for there cannot be any talk of the regeneration of a person if he does not utilize and develop his conscience. All programs and all statutes come from people and are intended also for them, and so on the conscience of people lies their content and the means of carrying them out. Unfortunately, there can be firm laws, there can be a faultless government, fair censorship, and fair police, in all forms, but they will not accomplish much if the citizens are without conscience. Dishonest citizens will get around all laws as it suits them, they will bribe the entire government, officials, they will betray their state, they will bind themselves to the last prison guard, and kill themselves to the last prison torturer, but there will be no one to punish the rest, and lawlessness will be supreme.

In this case, there is only one way out: in addition to a physical legal government which would utilize most progressive executives, there must also be a social and spiritual government which by its methods, bloodless methods, would reach to the deepest vitals of the human soul, where lies the human conscience. This is the best guarantee of the inviolability of the law. From the moment when the conscience of a person ceases to react, all laws become superfluous. In every state system, therefore, beside the physical administration, there must also be a moral and educational one.

The human conscience is a junction in the actions of the whole society. Religion sees in this its chief tool by which it raises morality and maintains it on a suitable level. The human conscience best knows how to differentiate good from evil, although, as some say, these are conditional concepts. Conscience is capable of greater or lesser sensitivity. No one can completely deaden it, even with the help of narcotics, in which more than one in the post-war period has been seeking counsel.

## EDUCATION FOR HEALTH AND PRODUCTIVITY

We live in times when statistics show that the number of nervously sick people are daily increasing. Among them are a large number of quite young people. Summarizing the testimony of physicians, it seems obvious that the cause of nervous diseases is that people are not living a proper, natural life, but an artificial one, which by its power has produced the present circumstances in which an insatiable craving for a constant increase of capital is dominant.

This immoral, unhealthy life more and more daily undermines the nervous system in a man; he becomes ill and, through heredity, he passes his illness on to his children in whom it acquires still greater force, thus, it passes from fathers to sons and grandsons. Therefore, from day-to-day, the human race deteriorates until, in time, there will be only abnormal people in the world instead of healthy ones. A second reason, for the numerous incidences of modern-day disorders, is that the food products are saturated with dyes and other chemicals, and many of the foods have been denuded of vitamins necessary to the organism.

A third cause is the improper education of children by their parents and the school. At the present time, too many parents do not train their children. Parents justify themselves by saying that they are overloaded with work and are unable to pay attention to their children. The school, in turn, often declares that its first responsibility is instruction, and that training belongs to the parents and non-school training organizations. This, of course, is a mistake of the present day school in that it has separated instruction from training.

One cannot imagine how teaching can be conducted without training and educating. Almost every insignificant movement of the teacher, while he is teaching children, is a movement that either trains or demoralizes the students. Certainly, the same thing applies even more so to the manner of speaking of the teacher, the phrasing of his thoughts and views. Not only in a long conversation but in every word he utters at a given time, he can either train or demoralize the students. Besides, one must not forget that youth is more observant than older people. An example of how some teachers do not want to train the students in the present schools can be seen from this, perhaps rare, authentic incident: In one school, during a rest-intermission, a small pupil about ten years of age stood two steps ahead of the teacher, took out a cigarette, lit it, and in the presence of the teacher and other older people smoked it. When he was asked what this meant, the teacher answered: "This does not concern me, it is the business of the parents: it is my duty to teach the English language, for I am paid for that and am held responsible for it by the administration. Parents should work less overtime and pay more attention to their children."

It is true that too many parents are working day and night, while their children are being educated on the street. However, the teacher has no right to ignore the questions of training in the way just cited. Every teacher, whatever his subject, must be responsible not only for the knowledge of his pupils but also for their conduct. It cannot be believed that a child who at an early age begins to smoke, will in the future, when he is an adult, be healthy.

Schools in which instruction is separated from training cannot be called ideal or even good schools. One is not free to forget that the teachers are training young people on whom will depend the future of this world. Houses of correction cannot do much if citizens do not place instruction and training in the schools on the proper level. Many of us feel the definite need for a reform of the school system. It must not be delayed. It must begin as soon as possible, for every day operates more and more to our disadvantage.

*Amusement as a Means of Intellectual Development*

The chief task of education is to develop alertness of thought and to be concerned with the correctness of mental inclinations. Practice, in the field of education, has shown us that work in school produces a system of thinking in the students and that their mental processes are strongly developed by well and wisely organized amusement. The school not only teaches a person how to think, but it spiritually forms a person in an extraordinary way; it polishes and endows him with those qualities of which only a person on a high standard of culture can boast. Good pastimes not only properly develop the mind but make the body and soul of a person healthy and make him optimistic and creative.

Looking into the history of education, one sees that, from ancient times, games and pastimes were practiced in the schools, for these were considered definite means for developing the ability to think and for developing the child physically.

With the coming of Christianity, games and pastimes were, to a certain degree, removed from schools, for then, more precise studies were introduced to make the mind more ready to recognize truth. In earlier days, the value of the body was put in second place, for there was the idea that, as the body grows strong, the mind of a person diminishes, i.e., deteriorates. In recent centuries, the school again returned to the ancient system and has been laying special emphasis on modern instruction in games and pastimes, for it considers them as one of the most important means for the intellectual and physical development of a cultured person.

The spirit of pastimes must not be separated from the spirit of art. But observing the amusements of the contemporary child, there cannot be seen in their pastimes anything that would have any similarity to art. Can it be called art when many little children of scarcely four or five years of age have each his own two toy revolvers and at every step aim them at a passer-by? It must be known that a weapon, such as a revolver, never was a weapon of honor, for such a weapon can be hidden easily and can be used to kill a person from ambush. It is very surprising that so many parents try to accustom their children to this weapon. Too often, as soon as the child can stand on his own feet, he begins to use toy guns, and the school often tolerates it. The school gives the impression that it is not its concern but that of the parents. Considering all this, one is not surprised by the somewhat too frequent cases which are published in the newspapers, where a small child kills someone, sometimes even his father, mother, brothers and sisters. This is nothing but the result of a faulty educational process that should have been foreseen when either the father or the mother first strapped those toy revolvers around the waist of a child.

## The Causes which Influence the Health of the Child Positively and Negatively

It is the sacred duty of parents to give as good health as possible to the child, so that he can live a happy, independent life and not be a burden to society. For a child to be physically and psychically healthy, one must pay attention to the primary causes on which health first depends. Very often, children are born sickly, and physicians very often attribute this to the parents who, through their imprudence or by not taking thought for the future consequences of their incorrect living, have become the cause of the misfortunes of children. Many cases of physically and psychically unhealthy children are found among people who habitually imbibe alcohol. Scientific circles often say that many intellectually undeveloped children primarily are the fault of their parents who too often and at unsuitable times have taken pleasure in alcohol. If parents wish to have healthy children, they must first wisely and carefully live their lives. This perhaps is especially true for the mother when the child is conceived or developing in the womb. How parents should live is carefully explained in gynecological literature, which should be read by those who wish to become parents.

The child must have appropriate care which includes abundant fresh air, a point that is often disregarded by the home, the school and community institutions. It is necessary to make every effort for the children to be as much as possible in the bosom of nature, for this produces a normal, healthy condition not only in the body but also in the psyche of the child.

Work also, in a great degree, aids in the health of a person, but only if it is carried on according to good hygienic principles. Reasonably organized work not only does not harm the health, but it facilitates the development of the will and character and develops the physical and psychic powers of a person. Very often, the lack of work injures a person physically and psychically. But work must be subject to certain norms and not to a planlessness which reflects only negatively on the physical and psychic structure of a person.

Psychological and physiological studies show that physical work generally exhausts a person more rapidly, but the fatigue from it passes comparatively quickly. On the other hand, intellectual work does not fatigue so rapidly, but the fatigue lasts much longer. It is wise to make frequent but brief interruptions in both physical and mental work. The best rest is to sleep. It is necessary to sleep during a definite time, for then the sleep will be deeper and will better refresh the person. The number of hours assigned to sleep depends upon the age of the person. The amount of time each person should sleep is discussed by Prof. Hryhoriy Vashchenko.[1] A suitable place is held by sports in the field of hygienic training, but one does not need to speak specially of these, for the school of today is overloaded with them.

*Education for Productivity*

In general, by productivity one means effective energy by which one begins and finishes a task. It must be the aim of every person first to desire, then to strive, and finally to apply all efforts to awaken his perhaps lethargic energy to activity.

It is the task of the school, and education in the broader sense of the word, to develop this awakened energy and to give it a corresponding direction in which it can best display itself, so that a person, from his youngest years, may properly become accustomed to fulfil his obligations and to feel his spiritual need to act in some useful manner, when he is fully adult.

The chief differences between a young person and an older one lie in the fact that the young person is constantly making new intellectual advances by the aid of uninterrupted intellectual processes and that memory in the young is more retentive. On the other hand, older persons acquire actual knowledge more easily, because they better know how to find the means for its clearer comprehension. Considering all the qualities of the individual disciplines, pedagogues have come to the almost unanimous conclusion that such subjects as mathematics, history, language, economy, and natural sciences are best taught to people while they are young, since the retentiveness of the memory is much greater in the young. Pedagogues also recommend the teaching of these subjects to the young, because through them the natural inclinations of the children are better revealed. All the senses should be developed during the formative years.

The present school aims to make the student productive in the shortest possible time. This succeeds when the teacher discovers the tendencies dominating in the student, awakens his faith in his

1. Vashchenko, Hryhoriy, *Tilovykhovannya yak Zasib Vykhovannya Voli i Kharakteru*, Munich, Druckgenossenschaft "Cicero" G.m.b.H., 1956, p. 50.

own powers, and rouses in him ambition for self-revelation and self-perfection. A person in this present era must analyze himself, he must ponder deeply and persistently. Those ages are past when a person lived in the bosom of nature, delighted and rejoiced in it. Cruel times are upon us, times of uninterrupted struggle and uninterrupted efforts to achieve a better way of life, a more productive and a more useful life. In the present era, a person dare not stop for an instant. He must proceed ever forward, otherwise, others will outstrip him.

The present times are cruel; they do not permit a person to lead a proper life. Materially his living scale is quite high, however, he has been forced to be machine-like in his activity, for he fears that, otherwise, he will lose his job and he and his children will perish from hunger.

The driving wheel of the present quest for production has acquired such speed that it cannot be slowed by these written lines.

In this terrible time, the philosophy of instruction and education only marks a few ways by which a person can keep himself in existence and, to a certain degree, have the right to call himself a human being.

A task of modern education, in developing a productive person, is to make him capable now of appreciating and foreseeing the beauty of life, for this alone will give him the desire to live and to strive. He must sense beauty in everything, especially in his mode of thinking, in his words, and actions. Every reasoning process must pass through the filter of criticism, and this mode of thinking must guard one against spiritual depression and keep him constantly in a proper spiritual equilibrium, which is most important in a cultured person. A psychically healthy person, even in very joyless surroundings, will still remain a person. His humanity at every step will dictate that he must have proper understanding and respect toward all. His progress will be such that, even under the most savage circumstances, it will break a path for a cultured person even through a spiritually-desolate jungle. Thus, his life will be much more possible and tolerable.

A further problem in the education of a productive person is making him useful. All the schools, beginning with the elementary schools and continuing through the universities, must try so to mold the individual that he will be completely useful, i.e., will know how to live, to be content with life, and, at the same time, not be an immobile log among other people.

Especially at the present time, one cannot permit obedience to the statement: Knowledge is for its own sake. Today, at every turn we must advance obedience to the directly opposite statement: All knowledge must be for life. So, regardless of the faculty in which a person studies — medicine, technology, or philosophy — no faculty is able to present its instruction in a manner which will make a person universal, but each of them must teach a modern man to think and live as modern times require. Otherwise, none of these faculties will be useful to any one, for it will function to the detriment of the individual as well as to the detriment of society. Therefore, every faculty must introduce that element, into its period of instruction, that will make the person versatile in life.

Considering well the life of a person at the present time, each of us will come to the conclusion that the centuries have passed when theoretical teaching could dominate. It doubtlessly gave great moral satisfaction and at the same time full material security to the individual. These centuries have been succeeded by a different time when only those theoretical disciplines dominate which have a wide application in practical affairs. In a word, at a fast pace, before our eyes, civilization is assuming supremacy over culture. This great impetus of civilization also will, in the future, strike the blank wall which it is building for itself, it then will rebound from this wall and will fall into an abyss. This terrible result can come in a very short time, but it also can tarry quite a long time. In those bitter hours that in their external form are opposed to real culture, which humanity has created during a whole millennia, a person yet will have to live who inwardly and spiritually still lived in those ancient times when not civilization but true culture flourished. An individual of this kind, at the present time, goes under and often perishes from hunger, for the world cannot value the creations of his soul and mind. Yet, it is essential to save people of this stamp and high qualifications for the future, for the future regeneration of culture will again sprout on the ruins of the present civilization. So we come to the conclusion that the modern intellectual man, who studies theoretical knowledge, who has sunk his roots only in culture, and has nothing in common with civilization, also must, besides his main calling, acquire another, more practical field, so that he may not die of hunger in the cruel present. We cannot think of any other device, because the psyche of modern society is different as are the categories of thinking.

So we feel more-and-more the need for a reconstruction of the system of human thinking, and it will certainly come. But who knows if it will not be too late?

## METHOD OF INSTRUCTION AND EDUCATION

Method, in the narrow sense of the word, is the means by which we examine definitely defined things, classify questions or events and perform definitely determined duties.

A broader definition of method first requires an understanding that nothing in life arose by virtue of its own essence but was produced by other causes which inspired someone to act or something to exist. In other words — in the broader sense of the word, method is a means of examining actual facts and the whole, real world.

The narrow definition of method faces up only to separated facts, examines merely some part of the whole situation; but each part, as such, cannot exist separately, because only in conjunction with other parts does it mark a definite whole. Considering this theoretically, we can engage in these abstractions, but we are not free to forget that these abstract elements are real life. Now comes the question: What method shall we choose in working in the field of education?

We have before us two kinds of method, one narrow and the other broad. The first has its application in partial instruction, i.e., in the study of a certain subject, and the other, the broader, takes into account education as a whole, i.e., its practical relations to the life of a man. The teacher must know both methods. For a psychologist's as well as for an educator's practice the narrow method is the interesting one. The second method, the broader, is on the road of life itself. The answer to the second and broader method will be dependent upon our attitude to different problems which will often enter our lives.

The quality of accomplishment of all actions is largely dependent upon the method. It is no more than a form of procedure; it is a tool with the help of which a person profits from some material or thing in properly performing some action. A method of instruction and education is nothing else, in its real essence, than a method which has some application in another action. Not only the teacher, but every artisan, in doing his work, does it by his own, already-practiced method.

This statement is important: Method in instruction must be based on the nature of a child, treating every child individually. A good teacher never imitates a tailor who cuts his material by a definite pattern. Method is not a clearly defined pattern which can be applied uniformly in the teaching and the educational process of every child. Before the teacher begins reflecting on the method, his first obligation is to look into the soul of the child, to analyze it, realize its character, and above all the child's temperament, and then apply individually the most suitable method to every child.

The quality of the method is also dependent on the subject of instruction. Every subject must be taught by a specially tested method. Thus, mathematics cannot be taught successfully by using a method which is applicable in the teaching of languages.

The first importance of method lies in the fact that, thanks to it, the children can absorb knowledge rapidly, intelligibly, and without a great struggle. The second importance of method is the systematization and the arrangement of the process of instruction. The author has known many people who have read a great deal; however, in talking with them, he at once felt that these people have worked a great deal upon themselves, that they have knowledge, but their fault lies in the chaotic condition of their knowledge, because they did not maintain a correct method during their studies. Instruction, without method, cannot give any one proper satisfaction, for, at every step, the teacher notices and the student feels that something is lacking.

Instruction, by a definite method, rests upon fundamental principles which make it lasting and valuable. The main point of teaching is to recognize the changes which arise in the mind of the child both as a result of instruction and of education. In recognizing the first changes, the teacher knows more-or-less how to conduct the next hours of instruction, so that after each class there may be a continuous further progress in the child's thinking. The understanding of all progress is the more important, for it blocks out the method for the further hours of instruction.

Many problems in the life of a person find their satisfactory solution in the method of his actions. One can recognize the importance of method by the eyes, the facial expression, and the bodily movements of a man when he encounters some difficulty which he must solve; he then seeks a method, for he regards it as a guide to a favorable goal.

In educational work, the teacher must introduce fresh thought as often as possible. This really is not method, but it is a direct necessity which is very important in the educational process. Fresh thought refreshes the educational method which embodies the law of educational activity. Freshness of thought brings enthusiasm into the school and makes the instruction interesting, pleasant, and optimistic. It also illustrates our real and intellectual activity, removes the children from dead formulae, which often have a minimum of application to the life of a person and insignificantly raise the level of his intellectual and psychic development. Teachers must not look at method through sleepy eyes; they must test it continuously and adapt it to the new mode of life.

A further importance of studies of method rests on such facts as: (1) It raises specific qualities; (2) It complements thought; (3) It organizes ideas; (4) It evaluates values; (5) It changes the memory; (6) It makes a person active, self-critical, and independent.

Knowledge in school must be connected with life, with actions, and it must function with the synthetic complexes of life rather than rely on classifications worked out by others. It must have a double goal: (1) to absorb prepared results; (2) to adapt and encourage the children to work, so that they themselves feel the need of discovering something new or, at least, to have the desire to reach what has already been discovered by others through experience. When instruction in the school relies upon the method of life, then the life in the school itself must be as similar as possible to the life of the whole society surrounding it. The school must embrace all its forms and chief problems which constantly and at every step enter life. It must possess in its vitals that order which is reflected at the time in the whole society, so that the student, when he leaves the school and enters life, does not feel strange in that social life but has a well-formed approach to the accomplishment of his individual tasks. In a word, it must be a creative school, a school of work, i.e., such as could enter life through life.

The old traditional school placed its psychological basis in the unusual capacity of the young mind. It sought for such conditions that forced the student in a model discipline to listen diligently. The teacher then could better pile more work on the passive students. The goal of education, in the present and future schools, should rely on making children capable of active reaction, and here it is necessary to emphasize the fact that active reaction is a means of intellectual development. In an active reaction, i.e., active in its attitude, a student of highly intellectual structure evolves. An important and basic item is that the educator and teacher first must teach in such a manner that the students will accept lectures with full interest.

One cannot consider favorably that system of instruction which overloaded the students with classroom work and unsuitably organized homework which, in turn, caused the evaluation of their knowledge to be incorrect. The teacher lectured or perhaps even noted an assignment in a book — "from — to" — "and you, little child, do what you wish at home, but learn it!" He evaluated by asking questions in class. He asked one student, and all the students had to pay attention; he set traps for those who guessed. Many nerves were strained by this testing, and the result was usually accidental. In some subjects the teacher tested very rarely, and when time was lacking, he merely evaluated the class by its appearance without asking any questions.

The object of education, in the new school, is that the teacher be guided only by the needs of the student. In such a case, he can become accurately informed about his students. If the teacher does not meet often with his students, he can and must strengthen his memory concerning them by notes, and records. Written homework should be limited to written summaries of lectures which the pupils should read aloud, and which, for exemplary verification, they should submit for criticism by the teacher. Care also must be taken that each lecture is based on life, so that the student will obtain the greatest value from it in the future, otherwise, instead of being a part of education, it will be quite the opposite, the deadening of the conscious and voluntary attitude and activity and, hence, the deadening of the student's personal ego.

A person constantly must see the object of his activity, otherwise, he has no desire and feels no need to sacrifice effort. Instruction which rests on only fulfilling dry rules is the worst type, but it is the easiest for the teacher. The teacher in this case does not need to know very many general laws; it is sufficient that he has mastered a small number of them and passes them on to others. But in order to know how to extract these laws from life and apply them to life, the teacher definitely must be acquainted with a large number of different cases which occur very frequently in life and are very often intertwined. He must know, and know practically, what to do in these cases; he must enter into the essence of all these things so as to understand the reason for these general laws.

So, the time is passed when we revealed knowledge in a flexible language and the time is come which demands from us not words but direct action. It is true, that many teachers frankly avoid questions, which are connected with practical actions, for practical actions evoke diverse phenomena, and these again are more interesting to the students. However, in connection with this interest, the teacher is showered with innumerable questions which he must answer, but to answer them he must work himself, he must study, and this does not suit everyone.

Activity is the specific quality of every child which can be seen best when the bell rings. Then, every child begins to live his own life, a life completely separate and independent. His gloomy face becomes radiant. The child demands movement because of his very nature, and the teacher must provide him with it, but he must direct it toward a good objective. The child actively must face the world of phenomena, for only then will he feel that he is truly living. The activity of his mind will become clearly aware of its tendency, and in following it he will find the confirmation of his existence.

Nietzsche is often not understood, but very often he is wrongly understood because of his great number of paradoxes. He rested the whole concept of his philosophy on the creative activity of the human spirit in regard to the world. He does not recognize good or evil as criteria of human morality. Instead, his criteria are greatness and indulgence. Under greatness, he understands creativity. He does not give recognition to a good man, only to a creative man. Everything that is not good, he understands as being something passive, unproductive.

We find the same in Leibnitz, especially when he deals with monads. A monad, of itself, gives its whole content. Its cause is external stimuli. It has no eyes, it always acts, and its activity lies in uninterruptedly clarifying the unclear ideas which it encompasses. Leibnitz continues with the classification of monads, divides them, and establishes a hierarchy. Every higher degree possesses a larger number of enlightened ideas. By movement, Leibnitz

understands eternal activity, activity which attempts more-and-
more to perfect itself. It does not seem strange why the old
theories were not able to change instruction in the schools, why
they did not take the active part of our souls into consideration.

We strongly feel that in many schools there is a lack of connection between instruction and the fullness of education. The
school, first of all, must be active in the fullest sense of the word,
for only then can it influence life. The school must consider the
character of the students, for the character is nothing else than the
awareness of activity, the voluntary choice of a goal. The school
does not take into account the character of the children and does
not train their character when it compels the children to work
without any choice of what children consider fitting. The system
of learning through doing is thoroughly natural, for it engenders
feeling and produces interest.

## Principles of the Educational Method

The method of instruction and education rests on the principles
of instruction and education. The importance of these principles
lies in the fact that on them is based not only instruction and
education, but they are the foundation on which rests all planning
of educational work in the narrow as well as the broader sense of
the word. Every theory, to permit its application in practice, must
rest on accurately worked out and accurately chosen terms. We
should make this demand of educational theory as well.

The principles of instruction and education are based on the
philosophy of education, and the philosophical theory usually is
confirmed by pedagogical practice. The educational principles are
many and explicable, which makes them clearly intelligible and
easy to comprehend. Very often, there are differences in regard
to the principles on which all the textbooks assigned by the state
mainly are based, but after consideration of these differences, the
deciding voice is that of the Department of Education, therefore,
upon it falls the responsibility for instruction and education in the
schools. The authors of educational textbooks always must comply
with the principles which aim directly for the objective which the
Department of Education has definitely set.

Very often, in the process of instruction and education, questions
arise to which there are no definite answers in the textbooks. In

these cases, discussion is permissible on the part of the pedagogical staff and on the part of students. However, the decisive results of the discussions, as to goal or method, cannot be at variance with the chief aim and the educational philosophy which the Department of Education accepted as its basis when it set forth the policy on instruction and education. In such cases, it is wise to seek advice from people who have had years of practice in this field and perhaps are better versed not only in educational philosophy but also in the philosophy of life which is encountered at every step and which must not be undervalued. In drawing up a program for education and instruction, the school always must have in mind that not only the most capable individuals who have already spent many years in this field but also those who have not had long practice must draw profit from it. Thus, the program must be worked out with applicability by all.

The chief task in erecting principles is to select a firm basis for concepts as well as guides for the individual in his relations to society. Every individual is an organism which at the same time embodies physical, psychic, and social life, and method in its broad sense must consider this threefold relationship. Therefore, every good interpretation must arise out of biology, psychology, and sociology.

The modern philosophy of education takes into account these three factors, and this is the first reason for its great educational process and its easy application in the process of instruction and education.

The main task of the life of a person is not only to maintain himself in life. He primarily must make every effort to progress in life, which can be accomplished not only by benefitting from his own experiences but also from those of other eminent individuals.

The process of experience is fundamentally a social value from the standpoint of biology, reason, and psychology. Peoples living a primitive life do not have definite social ties. With the growth of culture and civilization, each individual sees more clearly the need of close ties with the community, otherwise, he cannot profit by all the acquisitions of society. Society, even in very difficult and bitter economic and political situations, still finds a way for improvement, thanks to the qualified individuals which it picks for leadership from the commmunity. Moreover, the whole community makes every effort to acquire top level schools in which oncoming generations can always find suitable knowledge and without which they could, in no way, accomplish their technical and political tasks. The better developed the methods of education, the higher stands the educational work in a given state. These principles rest on deep theory and years of practice, and the range of their activity is very broad. The principle of instruction and education is the base of activity in the private life of all individual citizens, their families, and industrial and social groups.

The principles of instruction and education emerge from the life of a given nation, and they are primarily established for the present and future good of the people. Even their passive significance is equal to the active work of the teachers, administrators, and all the leaders of all activities, beginning with their inception and continuing to their conclusion.

When we speak of a difference of principles, it must be emphasized that principles which are devoted to the educational goal are somewhat broader than principles pertaining only to the instructional and educational method. The former also include principles of method, and, at the proper time, they are defined for the schooling and education of the given community. In analyzing the principles of instruction and education in different states, one comes to the final conclusion that the time has already come in which the work of instruction and education must rest on solid principles if we do not wish to see a catastrophic result in the educational system. But, if any one doubts this conclusion, he can convince himself very easily of its validity by visiting a school during recess or even classes during instruction periods where a person often wonders whether in these schools the instruction rests upon any principles.

There seems to be too much disrespect for the principles of instruction and education, because many people do not know that the proper education of an individual is at the same time a pledge for his properly good life, and they do not know that the first institution which best knows how to prepare the young for life is the school. It simultaneously assumes the great responsibility for the future of its students. This responsibility rests upon a suitable arrangement of the programs of instruction and education, on the practical carrying on of educational lectures, also, on the suitable arrangement and, above all, on the selection of educational material. However, in analyzing school textbooks, the schools often do not see in them deeply considered educational goals, although the authors of school textbooks certainly have devoted many hours to place the goal of education in the proper perspective therein.

In maintaining the position that a person in his early youth should live a happy life, i.e., should live happily in the present and not wait for happiness in the future, the school must not be a yoke into which a child is harnessed from his earliest years and must *willy-nilly* bear his burden. The school must be a second home for the young, therefore, the method of instruction and education in the schools must go hand-in-hand with the needs of the soul and body of the young. For the result of education to be good, all the conditions which enter into a given educational process must be made pleasant. Without corresponding conditions, the teacher and the student can never be able to achieve their goal. Modern educators strive for this first.

The essence of proper result in instruction and education lies not only in proper settings but also rests in the attitude toward the educational goal of teachers, students, and parents, but first of all it depends upon the resolutions of the government and the school administration. They first indicate the trend of the system of instruction and education by their resolutions and speeches, and so on them also falls the responsibility for any catastrophic condition in instructional and educational activity in the modern schools.

At the present time, it is necessary to emphasize at every step the importance of the system of instruction and education in the developing of a healthy nation. The school is the most important institution in the state. We are not free to treat it lightly.

*Factors in the Improvement of Educational Work*

All progress, whatever it may be, demands the continuous improvement of conditions. But the difficulties on the road to improvement are very great, and the teacher also encounters these in the course of his activity. In considering all the possibilities for the improvement of pedagogical work, we come to the one conviction that improvement first depends upon the innate capabilities of the individual teacher. For, in all cases which usually arise in the process of instruction and education, the methodology, although it might be very broad, cannot instruct. Generally, there is a conviction that the difficulties which occur in the process of instruction belong to the specific. One must not permit himself to forget that instruction and education cannot be separated from life, and the process of instruction and education must never be separated from the other processes which find their application in the daily life of a person.

In general, it can be said that there are three fundamental factors on which depends the quality of the result of any work:

1. The awareness of the object of the given activity which produces a definitely clear idea and all the reasons which induce the realization of the plans,
2. A clear understanding of the process arouses the desire to carry out the work as rapidly as possible to a successful conclusion,
3. The awareness of personal responsibility urges the completion of the task as well as possible. This is an essential part of every productive activity.

Awareness of purpose: The solution of the problems which rise in the life of a person is dependent first upon the clarity of the goal and the leading actions. A definitely determined goal in an action shortens the duration of the action and makes the result more effective. A person who undertakes an action must first know the quality of the material, what material to choose, and, also, what method to use which would best apply to the given material, to the circumstances, and to the time of year and hour of the day. In performing any action, one must not only know the goal but also all the reasons why we are striving to reach a higher goal. We might accomplish something because we see that our activity has brought some profit to others, or to ourselves, or we might do this because our work gives us pleasure which at the same time urges us to real activity.

The knowledge of principles and processes: From old times the human mind has dreamed of communicating with the planets. This idea constantly intrigued the minds of scientists, for awareness of the goal stirred them to think of it. But up to the present, no one found the way for such communication, because science had not yet established the principles and process of such a journey. Today, it is visible. This old hypothesis is becoming every day more of a firm theory, and in the not distant future interplanetary communication will come to be an ordinary thing. This action is steadily becoming more possible, for the human mind day-by-day is learning better the important laws on which fully depends the achievement of these conceptions.

The feeling of personal responsibility: In addition to the above discussed factors, there is one more factor on which depends in a large measure the achievement of the goal, and that is the feeling of personal responsibility. In our daily life, it can be noticed best how important this factor really is. We often see very capable people, very good artisans, very good physicians; yet people approach them with great caution, although they know that they are better craftsmen than others, because unfortunate incidents occurred which have warned people and taught them to be distant with these individuals, for they very often refuse to be responsible for their work.

The importance of this last factor is best seen in individuals who take part in some leading group, and it is noticed no less in work which a person does almost automatically. It should be the desire of every individual to rise spiritually above an automaton. The workman must know not only the process, but he must act in the consciousness of his responsibility. All these factors appear in every, even, almost imperceptible act. We must remember that these three factors in our awareness do not appear separated nor do they need appear in the order given. The sense of obligation and of personal responsibility in individuals often occurs at the beginning, before the undertaking of the work, while knowledge of the process begins somewhat later.

Knowing the weight of these factors and their necessity for every action, it must be underlined that they always appear in the instructional and educational work of a teacher. If the effective act in all individual situations is dependent upon the awareness of these factors, a teacher probably requires it even more during the realization of his instructional and educational activity. There is realization that the ideas of the teacher must have an imperative character, because both instruction and education enter into the broad region of human actions, the goals of which are often intertwined. Moreover, the leading features of these very different forms very often exist unnoticed, which makes it very difficult to differentiate their essential elements. Yet, although this activity, this work of a teacher, is not easy, teachers are all of the conviction that, with each new day, they will see ever more effective work in the field of instruction and education, for every student will consciously approach and undertake his work.

The work of instruction and education is difficult also, because there is now a period of great development of civilization and, especially, of narrow specialization; therefore, instruction must go hand-in-hand and adapt itself to the new conditions. This work, in many cases, is very complicated and often it is only with great difficulty that teachers can hold to the given factors, for the great quantity of different aspects.

The situation, in the field of education, can be closely compared today to a landscape: stand far back from the subjects which impress us by their charming form and color, and we see only their beauty and we rejoice in it. But when we approach quite near, that beauty will escape our eyes like an illusion and, in its place, there will come something real, something accurately defined. We see the weird forms of the crags and the dangerous abysses of the earth, which similarly form the daily work of the teacher amid a like nature. And this beautiful nature is reminiscent of the various kinds of instruction and education. In this case, teachers must look at instruction and education only from a great distance, otherwise, they will not understand its significance. Later, the teacher approaches nearer and nearer and very often comes in contact with very weird facts, like mountain crags, but, relying on his own resources, he begins to hew and later to polish the still somewhat cruel nature of the young people.

### The Need for Theoretical Knowledge

Theoretical knowledge is the first prerequisite for well-accomplished actions. The physician could not begin to cure a sick person if he had not had proper theoretical preparation. The engineer could not build a machine if he did not have a good knowledge of mathematics. Likewise, not one of us can begin a discussion if he does not know the main bases of logic. Therefore, all our work must begin with theory and later pass to practice if we wish to achieve a good result. The history of instruction and education shows this most clearly.

The theory of education reaches its roots as far as does the roots of the human race. Even in the times of the most primitive life of men, there was already a theory of education. This old theory was not in books, but it was implanted in the soul of every mother who told her child what to do, but before that she told him why he should do it a certain way. Even when a person begins to work practically, theory exists in a greater or lesser degree, but it is more difficult to recognize, because the method is different and strange.

Furthermore, the task of education is not only to make a person capable of coping with life, but it is not a less important mission to implant in the soul of the child all the principles through which a person becomes a true person.

The concept of universal education was created by the necessity which is produced by the gap between the life of a child and the life of an adult. But it is known that we cannot consider as good many things done by adult people. Thus, the school, which is responsible for the education of the young, must control the life of the young not only within its walls but also outside of them. In this manner, the school constantly reshapes the young souls and encourages them to constant progress in a properly good direction. This unceasing work calls for a corresponding illumination of the goal and of all values which educational theory first gives. Very often, humanity has many different inspirations for generous deeds, but these are irretrievably lost because they do not fit into its own actual trend. It is the task of the philosophy of instruction and education to teach the teachers and the parents not to disregard important phenomena in children, but to exert their efforts so that their children can translate their ideas into noble actions.

It is generally believed that life is constant progress in which a person grows physically, rationally, and psychically. At the same time, he continuously perfects his preceding accomplishments, so that through their aid he can create new goals for his future tasks, gain new ideals as well as new opportunities. Thus, a person works without interruption and becomes valuable in the utilitarian sense of the word. His life becomes valuable and thus fully differs from a wild and uncivilized life. It can be seen that progress of this kind is found within the walls of the school. By studying different subjects, with the help of different methods, the child daily grows physically, mentally, and spiritually, for with every day he understands better-and-better the value of life. The ideal of spiritual growth means the constant development of all resources, to which the aim of theoretical instruction can be of greatest assistance.

## EXPERIENCE AS SUCH

The term "experience" is used generally in the analysis of all physical and psychical events. Thoughts or ideas, feelings or emotions, aspirations for work, and the activity itself are closely connected in the process of experience. One must not identify experience with knowledge, for knowledge covers too small a field. It does not contain the elements of dexterity, accuracy, and productivity, considering all these terms in their usual sense. Knowledge and ability are synonyms, for, very often, one might be able to accomplish some work, but the difficulty lies in the fact that one does not know where to begin it because of lack of experience.

### The Nature of Experience

The nature of experience can be defined by saying that it includes active and passive elements specifically combined. Understanding what is meant by activity, one understands what is meant by endeavor, the meaning which certainly is connected with the term "experience." Understanding the meaning of passivity, one understands memory, feeling. So when we bring anything into our experience, to a certain degree we sustain and we learn the consequences of the result. Thus, every act definitely evokes a counter-act.

Prominent pedagogues see a reciprocal relation between action and reaction, between the organism and its environment. Herbart made a distinction: he called the relation of a person to objects experience, and the relation of a person to a person a relationship.

In the pragmatic philosophy of education, the act of thinking is a direct movement toward a goal, toward the solution of problems. This act strives, as rapidly as possible, to find the guides and thoughts which are necessary for the solution of practical difficulties.

Thought is a tool; an idea is something basic. When it is a question of a knowledge of nature, our knowledge is based first on observation and not immediately on experience, as for example in the case of astronomical sciences. Hence, thinking is a pure reflection of one's own philosophy but, at the same time, it is a power which demonstrates itself by its conclusions. The corresponding union of these two phases of experience, i.e., action and counter-action, is, at the same time, a measure of the value of all experience. Experiences, as tests, evoke various changes, but they are very often only a crossing of our thought, which is absolutely uncon-nected with the returning moments of counteraction. When the action continues and when by the strength of the fact we are compelled to recognize the result, our action is intersected with a valuable meaning. In no case can we call it experience when a child, without thinking, puts his hand between the cogs of two wheels. Experience comes when the counter-action is the result of our conscious action.

Experiences form in our mind the mirrors of time and space, which are connected with objects in the external physical world. However, inclinations for various transitions from one thought to another are features of the structure of the mind which we have from birth; we can perceive their growth, and we can also see how every succeeding experience profits from the successes of the former, so that this chain of experimental actions creates an order of experiences in time and space, connects phenomena, thus, creates an actual cause of all the forms of our thinking.

All this, taken together, is our education, our training. Our training is our greatest friend and aid, for it helps us constantly by the fact that it is available for real and definitive use. A person with experience will accomplish his task with greater success and in a shorter time. The reason is that experience is the knowledge of separate cases, while knowledge, in the general sense, is the understanding of general principles. If anyone has theory without experience, or has knowledge but does not know the chief principles on which it is based, he will always make mistakes, for he will not know how to adapt this knowledge to separate cases.

We must never think that skill is a quality of knowledge and not of experience, nor should we consider a person who has only knowledge wiser than the one who has experience. A person with proper experience accurately understands a fact. But if he has only knowledge, he knows only the cause of the fact. We consider knowledge a higher form, for everyone who possesses it can transmit it in greater or lesser amount to another person, but experience can never be transferred to another; each person applies it to the extent he acquired it in life.

Considering the questions connected with our experience, it

becomes clear why physical realism has such a wide application in the modern world of today. Its importance lies in the fact that it furnishes us objective activity in regard to all our concepts, which have their real existence in the objective world.

Very often there is complete disorder in our thoughts, because of the various views which daily acquire more authority in the world. According to these views, we must regard as real only the world as explained by physical terms.

And so, summing up the results of the considerations of various tendencies, we come to these conclusions: that the world, which is usually considered in the natural sciences, is but an idealized world; it is a spiritual world in which its spiritual values have their great application in everything. We recognize the great value of spiritual treasures when we classify them. None of them is separate, but they are organically connected with one another and together form a great and very valuable tool which leads us to an honorable and properly correct life. These hidden, spiritual values broaden our intellectual vision which in turn properly and beneficially formulates our actions and efforts.

We then live a truly human life, when we agree to have all our thoughts realized by this spiritual actuality. Spiritual actuality is able to inspire everything that has any relation to language, literature, art, knowledge of our mutual relationship, and to everything that we call culture and even civilization.

The spiritual world gives us new conceptions of time, in truth not by the way that mathematical reality gives them, but as a progressive realization of spiritual actuality. So it is perfectly natural that the world of our experience, the world of thoughts and intellectual efforts also correctly should be a world of spiritual values. Thus, because of everything that we see around us at all times, death, psychic chaos, wars, we are not able, at the same time, to see the real picture of the true world, i.e., how the world looks in its spiritual features.

Taking into account experience in the broad spiritual sense, it is an uninterrupted struggle in which we unceasingly realize our life and active spiritual oneness, which is always with us but can also be without us in space and time. The revelation of the reality of this active, spiritual oneness is the task of philosophy. We would feel a great loss and even a defeat if we resigned from this struggle, for we would then lose sight of our spiritual bond which joins ancient times with the present and the future.

*Experience in the Hours of Instruction*

Very often we see in some gymnasia that only one tendency of the individual was trained without any attention being given to the wholeness of the soul, and this method of training pertains to subjects which are not connected with life, but to purely abstract subjects. The results of the system are that the institution trained a young generation which is insufficiently developed for life, without the benefit of any experience. This is a situation to which the words of Montaigne apply: "What is the profit when a child wastes fifteen or sixteen years on this kind of instruction in school. Would it not have been better had the child spent these years playing with a ball, for at least his body would have profited."[1]

Yet, no one wants the school to return to nature in the popular sense of the word, or to so-called pseudo-nature, but we must collect truly natural phenomena and group them according to the goal that we have set. Yet, in order that the theory expounded be not problematical, but stable, it must be established on the firm principles of experience carried out in the presence of the children. Such experience is extraordinarily useful in its results.

Someone can argue that such a system requires great effort and even involves material expenses. This is easily understandable, for the better, the more solid, the more finished the system, the greater material expenses will it involve. The cheapest type of teaching often is, at the same time, the poorest. The material argument is no argument, for through it we can in no way justify the irresoluteness of the teachers and the ignorance of the students.

As a proof that theory must rest upon experience we can cite the words of Herbart. He compares experience to a broad plain where the eye observes every object which is on the plain, while theoret-

1. De Montaigne, Michel Eyquem. *"Essais."* Paris, Librairie Garnier frères, 1948, vol. III.

ical instruction he compares with only a slender thread which trembles with every sound of a bell.[1]

To refuse experience is the same as to refuse the light of the sun and be satisfied with the light of a small lamp. The postulate of experience is no new postulate. It rests on the statements of such experts of science as Locke, Rousseau, Herbart, Pestalozzi, Komensky, and even Aristotle. They say that our imagination must be as clear as possible and that only on clear imagination can clear understanding be built. Yet, here we can meet with the psychological objection which maintains that comprehension can arise when based on merely one representation or figure of the imagination, but can anyone guarantee that this will not produce a false comprehension in the soul of the child, i.e., one that contains completely false elements.

In considering the question of experience, it can be cited that, in an hour of instruction in one of the European schools where the teacher of geography mechanically moved his hand around the map, describing the mountain ranges and their character, and made every effort to interest his hearers, the words came out from his mouth without any spirit. After some time, everyone knew that this teacher had been born and educated in a place where there were no mountains, and this was the reason why his lecture cast his audience into the arms of Morpheus.

The situation is no better in some schools in the teaching of languages. How much effort has a teacher made with the accent and pronunciation, how much energy has a teacher put forth so that his students would imitate him and master the accents of a language. Unfortunately, it turns out that the instruction was incorrect, that it did not agree with the rules of the literary language because, the teacher, in learning a foreign language, perhaps English, never during his studies had the opportunity to hear the true, literary, English language from the lips of an Englishman, which is why the teacher speaks it incorrectly. This proof is confirmed by every emigrant who has himself experienced how incorrectly the English language was taught, and it would have been better if those hours assigned for this instruction would

1. Herbart, Johann F., *Allgemeine Pädagogik und Umriss pädagogischer Vorlesungen*, Leipzig, Siegismund & Volkening 1876, bl. 127.

have been used, as said before, for ball-playing, for it would have made his body stronger.

Experience in any field, after all, is completely different from the acquisition of observations and, if so, it must be an independent procedure, and it will be exhaustive if the observations are exhaustive. Impressions and sensations are developed into observations and, when we appeal to one of the senses with the aim of developing an observation, we must be certain that the preceding experience exhausted the impression. It is only in this way that one spark evokes another and this a third, and so it creates a complete observation.

The task of education is to give new sensations to experience which are connected with a subject. The fuller the circle of impressions, the clearer, stronger, and more durable are the observations. One can see this best in children; a child is never satisfied with an object only by seeing it, but he insistently tries to touch it with his hands or even tries to eat it.

Thus, before the teacher can build up concepts and judgments, he must enrich the students with a great number of representations (figures for the imagination), which can be accomplished more quickly and perhaps even more completely by arousing interest. In order that more interest be engendered, there must be a stronger link between the elements from which the phenomena of life arise, for broken and isolated elements will not arouse interest and, therefore, the phenomena cannot be understood. Teachers must, therefore, try to follow a natural path to arrive at the most complicated discoveries, and only the person who reaches a definite goal by this path will be able to return to his first position, i.e., he will be able to apply the theory which had been set forth to life.

When we speak of experience which goes hand-in-hand with activity and the evocation of various changes in the real world, then, on the other hand, intellectual recognition is joined into a whole with practical actions. And it is this last step that the school tears off from its natural wholeness and postpones its use to the adult years of its students. Thus, such a school does provide some store of knowledge, but this knowledge is detached. Furthermore, the school considers that those general laws which every student knows by heart will be very easy to adapt in practical life — in practical reality.

But this question has a completely different aspect, for the students often not only do not know how to apply these laws to life, but often they even do not imagine that it is possible to apply these laws in practice. The school often does not care whether this spiritual food with which it feeds its students is proper for them, whether they will profit by it; in a word, the school often does not consider the nature of the students, which Rousseau considered as the chief criterion. Such schools do not consider the human dignity of its students, for they do not know the object of their activities.

Perhaps, this development of interest through practical action is placed last in some schools or is completely lacking, because the schools first wish to emphasize the great significance of pure knowledge, but we must realize that if we reject the development of interest through practical action, we are, likewise, not training creative interest in the realm of theory.

Many teachers stick so closely to the textbooks that we can guess that their knowledge does not greatly exceed the dry material which is found in the textbooks. And very often, their knowledge does not have any connection with life, and, therefore, their knowledge cannot overcome impediments in their own life, for it does not come from life. The productive method also is completely foreign to many present-day modern teachers.

Now, when the teachers come to the crux of the matter and begin to analyze similar hours of instruction, they must justify to the students their insufficient knowledge of the material. It is scarcely possible for a teacher to impart knowledge if it is only appended to the teacher, because without practice it could in no way enter the bone and the blood of the students. It is not difficult to learn something and to transmit it to another, but it really is difficult for the learner if he cannot derive the theory from life and adapt it to life.

The application of practical activity in the school is not a whimsical expression of some trite pedagogical convictions, it is an inescapable need of the present and still more of the future years. There was a time when there was no interest in questions of production, for the desire was to raise the school to the heights of theoretical interests, but the school cannot rest only on theory without practice, for theory without practical application loses in value, and the practical benefit of such teaching is not very great.

In pleading for practical activity in the schools, it should not be understood by this that schools must be overly concerned with material benefits. Rather, they should be concerned with striving to make a child capable of facing life. In addition, practical actions in a school attract the children and make them ready to work. At the same time, practical instruction is retained. It can be explained that the retention of knowledge is secured in this way. Students are compelled to become interested in the phenomenon, for instructions are often repeated in their work, which is really the reason why a given phenomenon grows integrally into the identity of the child. It is true here that the degrees of achievement in knowledge are diverse, but there are no such great deviations as in theoretical instruction. Furthermore, the need for experience is evident at every step.

Every level of progress strives for a more perfect order than did the preceding, a better system of actions, and a more concrete direction. One can hardly imagine a progressive, modern life without suitable laws, ethical regulations, and proper procedures. Everyone sees, in practical life, the importance and necessity of a system and of order, necessary not only in private but also in social activities. Achievements and even life are fully dependent upon the degree of a so-called practical routine and a capacity for life.

But we cannot think of progress if we exclude all possible changes. In all progress and during great changes, a moment of slight pause is desirable for making new decisions and chiefly for controlling the directions of change so as less to endanger the quality of the result of these uninterrupted steps of progress. This need for controlling the system, even in periods of rapid changes, absolutely is necessary. Thus, civilization is assuming those forms which experience guarantees and gives all due respect to constant modifications.

So, with the progress of culture and civilization, there is a definite need to accept a new form and system of instruction and education, for it appears that this present system is already outmoded or was not properly arranged even from its very beginnings.

With the progress of humanity, the development of civilization and the growth of interest in nature, the need for new, basic changes in the educational system rises more-and-more to the surface and becomes ever more evident. Not only the school but other social institutions as well show similar efforts to submit themselves to forms of practical experience and the achievements of progress.

Such important institutions, in which experience plays a large role, (such as the school, or even those where the method of practical experience has a broad field for the demonstration of one's abilities, such as social institutions) must exist not only primarily for themselves, but their existence can be justified only if their great experience satisfies the life needs of the modern progressive individual. *Already, the last hour has come when, without long reflection, we must ask educational reformers to enter the walls of the schools and other institutions and make them more applicable to the present era and the demands of a cultured and civilized person.* The reformers of the educational system will take as their starting point all possible criteria which adherents of the present educational system will suggest to them. All changes which they will make in this direction will closely bind the present with the past, and, at the same time, the present with the future.

In the process of improvement, the experiences of the past are always taken as the starting point, and they are only supplemented with the experiences of the present and modified for the probable demands of the future.

Every individual possesses a definite relationship to his own past and future; he is also in a very definite relationship with the social milieu, as an inalienable part of it. Every child must live in the future among social institutions, such as churches, libraries, schools, etc. Under these circumstances, in order that his life might be agreeable and profitable for all, we must include this element of education in the program in introducing a reform of the educational system.

In the very term community, education is included as an essential link between its members. It is included in all the qualities which fall within its scope as well as with all the circumstances in which it develops its noble activity.

In general, growth is renewal and the perfecting of experience, which simultaneously mark the development of better living conditions in both the material and spiritual sense. It can be said that a truly noble person, even though he has great material and spiritual abundance, will never be satisfied by them if he sees that his environment is in extreme need. Analyzing these written in heavy print on such an authoritative science in this field as psychology, we come to the convincing conclusion that the world must improve, it must be reborn and made more worthy to receive the results of the progress of culture. It must be so arranged that people of all classes and of all races living together will live in harmony, which would in no way dare to allow even the slightest noticeable dissonance that might, in turn, again disturb the chords of the heart of a true person.

We note, by this noble rebuilding of the world, certain signs: the modernized world will produce a new type of person who will have true freedom as the most noticeable means of revealing his own self. This freedom is like the motivating power of psychic sensations and is the chief rudder for its noble aspirations. This freedom is a path through the dense thickets of bitter state or customary laws. It is something which stands above laws, for freedom in this understanding, by its natural nobility surpasses even those noble individuals who created true human laws. Freedom is the revelation of all intellectual and spiritual powers which by their gigantic growth have destroyed all inhuman manifestations, so that they themselves could grow for the good of individuals and society. The existence of ideal freedom, uncontrolled by legislation or enforcement by a government, in the future, will be realizable fully if the teachers now begin teaching not only the children but all citizens to understand correctly the term freedom.

Under reform of the educational system, one must understand not only reform of the educational system in the schools or in educational institutions, but also educational reform in the broad sense of the word. The school must first teach the community to understand correctly the meaning of so-called democratic freedom. Freedom must be understood as permitting everyone the right to reveal his thought and to exert influence for appropriate changes in the efforts of the government. In the further conception of freedom, every individual should have the right to arrange his life to his own liking, to have his own standard of living and, at the same time, have his own method through which his life becomes easier and more pleasant.

But democratic freedom does not consist of advantages for only one member of society, without taking into account the same rights for the other members of society for as pleasant a life as possible. Freedom for the individual reaches as far as it does not cross its boundaries and does not cause trouble for other members of society. The individual, as a member of the community, has the right to express his opinions, but the same individual has no right and must even be punished if he rejects ordinances which concern other people's rights, hygiene, the cultured appearance of public buildings or public property. Contempt for the regulations of the state government does not fall within the scope of democratic freedom in any way. In a democratic state, people must be guided, if necessary, compelled along the rails of culture and civilization. A member of the community must know that if some trash or used paper bothers him in his own pocket, he will annoy his fellow-citizens even more if he litters the sidewalks or streets.

In some democratic states, the freedom of children in the schools perhaps is also wrongly understood. The author, here refers to cases where children are given excessive freedom with the argument that it is desired that the children better show their attitudes toward the given disciplines, for then the teacher has the chance to find the best approach to the student and at the same time opportunity to waken in the student his latent but innate capabilities.

Freedom should not mean that the student has unlimited freedom over which there is no legal control. The student must have freedom only in the range of his demonstrated interest, but it must not pass beyond the frame of educational discipline, or it would be impossible to imagine any teaching or education. For example, it is right to reject any privilege of students which would give them freedom of movement to smoke cigarettes during or outside the hours of instruction and completely ignore the rules of his teacher or other adults. It is not strange that schools with a less liberal education often have much greater success in the teaching and educating of truly intelligent students.

In the reform of the school system, some believe that a law should be included obligating youth of the secondary schools to wear a uniform to make it possible to control their lives outside of school. Teachers must, at all cost, remove from the schools and from educational institutions the totally stupid practice of foolish imitation. Because one student does something, his friends, looking at him, do the same thing; when asked why they are doing it, no one knows how to answer. One can see this same practice in some doers, when a believing person will spend whole hours kneeling and praying, but when a poor man asks for five cents for a piece of bread, instead of getting the five cents, he will be answered that helping the poor is the work of the government and the Salvation Army. So at every step, we note the lack of proper thinking and the lack of understanding of the essence of religion and of the educational system.

The future should bring equal treatment of all the inhabitants of a given state. Without a proper, human treatment of all the residents, there cannot be a happy life for that state. In disregarding this question, all reforms will be only a worthless expenditure of time and money. Every reform, and above all the reform of the educational system, must be based on just, human laws which protect and safeguard every person without regard to what social class one belongs, or to the race or birthplace of his forefathers. Once he is a resident in a democratic state, he must have all the rights not only in theory but also in practice which will fully insure his freedom and equal rights and at the same time will contribute toward his happy life. If we do not wish to introduce reforms in this question, it is better not to permit people from other states to enter our state for if a people living on the territory of its own state does not admit foreigners into its circle and on equal terms, in a short time, they will be changed from the best of friends into the worst of enemies, and their hostility toward the state will be much more intense, for they will be enemies within the given state.

The necessity of introducing a reform of the educational system becomes increasingly evident, and in the present conditions, it is the only means which psychically can improve the health of the nation in a very short time.

The conception of general social progress, which can be realized by the creative progressive possibilities of a person, must also consider all the criteria in formulating the educational program in the broad sense of the word. We can foresee some difficulties which will be stumbling blocks in the path of the educational reformers. All opposing views will make every effort not to allow these reforms to be introduced, but in the interest of the entire people of every state, the process of educational rebirth must be accelerated, for the more rapidly a nation is reborn spiritually, the better for it and for the state government.

Constant regeneration and constant improvement are at the essence of this world, and not only of humanity. One knows from physics, biology, and psychology that such good action in the world constantly exists and that it is indispensable; if we hinder it, we act against nature, against which man is incapable of winning in such a conflict. The nature of the universe and the nature of man were not always as they are today. Many billions of years passed before the world assumed its present form. In the world, uninterrupted changes constantly are occurring. Constant transitions, constant growths which rise from something already antiquated and useless, grow again, manifest themselves in something entirely new, which is gladly accepted.

In no code is there a law which forbids evolution, and so we must not try to stop evolution in the field of education. Man, as the wisest creature, must emerge from the closed centuries of the underground of antiquity by the power of the natural light of his reason; he must build life for himself on the surface in the light of theoretical sciences and experience, a life which would fully reflect his humanity.

The methods and trends of all the actions of man can be good for one person but completely repulsive to other individuals, and they can also very often be inappropriate for the same person in other circumstances. The character of experience must be chosen, and a person must complete the act of choice, for he is material out of which can be fashioned only one form, and the quality of the form is at the disposition of the free will of the person.

All social institutions must show greater interest in the reform of instruction and education; they simultaneously must make every effort to make their members properly satisfy the demands of a future reformed system. The cooperation of all educational institutions will facilitate the carrying out of the reform. As is done to a child in school, it is necessary to accustom the adult citizen of the community to do good instead of evil. Democratic freedom does not mean that a person must have freedom in the absolute sense of the word, and that all the unregulated tendencies of his nature cannot be regarded as evil deeds, for these must always be punished if the law of justice is to be maintained.

The idea of individual freedom emerged in the struggle against violence and tyranny. That condition which had its place in ancient times has now been changed into something quite opposite, because violence and contempt for human dignity was and is against natural law on which all laws should be based. This abrupt change under the slogan of absolute freedom of man also produced great changes in industrial and social establishments, advancing the concept of natural freedom and equality to the prime position.

The idea of the freedom of the student, which lies in the broad range of the freedom of man, must also undergo certain changes and limitations. The question of individual freedom in lecture halls and outside of them must be so presented that it is in harmony with the spirit of rational freedom, that is, freedom which rests upon the criteria of the mind and not on the reflexes of the unreasoning whims of a child and his sensations. In the concept of freedom there is involved a choice of one's goal and the means to achieve it, yet, everyone, whether a child or an adult, is responsible for all the actions which he has taken relying on his own free will, unforced by any external compulsion.

The objective of the new system of instruction and education is that control of the children in their class work and in behavior so that every child would himself feel the responsibility for fulfilling his obligations properly. The child must have the possibility of choice in the new educational system. Until now, in the schools of some states, the child in the secondary school has had the right to choose cooking or typewriting or driving an automobile instead of algebra, for he thought that algebra or some other subject was too difficult and he did not want to exert himself to that extent. But the freedom of a child should not be permitted to extend so far. The freedom of a child must extend only to the point where he has the right to make a choice between a secondary school for general education and some trade school which is easier, less exhaustive; but a child must never have the right to make changes or choose between subjects which have been properly thought out and appropriately set forth in the program of instruction of a given school. Thus, the child has the right to choose the school but not the subject.

### The School as a Source of Experience

Education, as an ordinary individual fact, means the sum of all changes and the influence of the surroundings in all directions, not only in the best sense of the word but also in the worst. Changes very often take place in a nation without the slightest plan, quite accidentally, without following a planned direction or a proper leadership. One must not then be surprised that such changes have an undesirable effect.

Organizations, social groups, and institutions should try not to permit the progress of their members to assume an accidental course. They should make every effort to assure that a definitely defined progress should guide their members to a goal previously approved by the leaders. The more so, because the ideals of different organizations differ as do the ideals of individual groups and institutions. The aim of spiritual progress or of the so-called spiritual changes in the members of an organization is that the given organization attempts to make its members spiritually capable of attaining the goal set by the leadership. However, the importance of the work of the leadership is not completed only by the choice of a proper ideal to which its members should aspire; its task is also to find appropriate ways to apply the efforts of the members of the organization.

Practice has shown that the same ideal can often be achieved by a correct course, but, very often, it is harder and longer, despite the fact that certain individuals achieve this ideal by a much shorter and simpler route, but this is often contrary to natural and written law. Political, religious, industrial, and social systems try not to allow the spiritual development of members of their organization to proceed at random.

Even taking it historically, the school has always provided the community with new, selected, young members for leadership through its long inculcation of ideals. From the beginning of its existence, it performed its work very solidly, and no other educational organization could ever equal it in this aspect.

Furthermore, demands made on a school by separate organizations very often are contradictory, and the administration of the school is often in a very unpleasant position, for it does not know which of them to satisfy. In such a case, the school does not dare to consider the demands of any one organization, but it must choose for its course that direction which everyone would call just. The school must know that its chief goal is the continuous betterment of the experience of the students and all other functions of the school in this case must be secondary. The ideals and aspirations of individual groups which make efforts to influence the schools are quite imprudent compared with the main goal of the school: the making of every effort that the children will every day become more and more experienced. The selfish demands of the individual groups or organizations, as to the work of the school, have very often not been carefully considered. Leadership of the school must in no way take them into account.

The antagonism of some party or of some other tinge must not be introduced within the walls of the school. The school is a second sanctuary, thus, it cannot have room for any partisan quarrels. No group or no party can dare to dictate its principles to the leadership of individual schools. The school first must strive to prepare the young properly for life, must teach the children to live in varying circumstances, which can be achieved in two ways:

1. When it will view education in the schools as preparation of the young for previously outlined future life;
2. When it will try to insure that the child lives a full and pleasant life now, at the present time, and that he knows how to satisfy all the demands of modern conditions.

When we adopt criteria and on their basis try to judge something after having first determined whether it is good or bad, we come to the conclusion that a given thing can be good and can simultaneously be bad, depending upon the object the thing is going to serve. If it is destined for a good purpose, it will be good, and if for a bad purpose, it will be considered bad. When we accomplish a good goal but make use of evil means, then our work will be completely evil. To differentiate accurately what goal is good and what means to reach that goal are good, a person must have, at least, some experience, and, here, in the first place, the school is the basis of experience.

Returning to the nature of the educational process, or rather to the educational experience, it must be underlined that every experience has its beginning in the organic demands of a person; it is achieved either to his satisfaction or the demands are merely transitory, because of the exhaustion of the organism. A person always tries to do what now best suits him, or at least, he hopes that it will bring him satisfaction in the future. Here, the question arises as to how he should proceed so that what he does can be called good. This is true especially if we take into consideration the fact that the world, that is, science, the state order, and everything else, greatly progresses every day, and what was good yesterday, today may be completely bad. The question rises: On what criteria is the judgment of our daily actions to be based?

It is true that the world is changing every day, but its changes are not in substance but in quality. The essence both of the macrocosm (the universe) and the microcosm (the individual) is order which is unchanging. This order is unchanging in the universe and it is also unchanging in the individual. At the same time, today, we can freely say that there is no power in the world that can change this order, and even more to the point, there is no person who can change it, because it is not dependent on the will of a person.

In the worst case, a person is able to destroy our earth but not the universe. A person also is not able to destroy that order which he possesses. He is able to destroy himself, i.e., the thing within which this order rests, but he is not able to destroy the order itself. This order places him on a proper pedestal, it separates him from other creatures, it dictates to him what he should do and what he should not do, it always reminds him that he is a rational animal. Therefore, we should not be frightened by the great changes taking place on our earth. Our task is to maintain order which was the same at the creation of the world and will remain the same to its end, the only change will be that of its external form, or, rather, its appearance, but these changes are only qualitative. We must maintain order in all circumstances, and how to do so must be taught by the school.

Now we see how necessary good leadership and control is in the school. The need of good guidance for the school grows with every day. Now everyone feels the need for a renewal or even the complete rebuilding of the educational system in the schools, for the further it goes, the more difficult it will be to reform the school. It seems that too many people do not notice the mistakes of the present school, or they consider them a necessary evil. But those who are interested in the life and work of the young in the schools see that the young people profit less every day from a school if it is drying up more-and-more and is ceasing to nourish the young with its life-giving juices. The mistake of such present schools is found in their planning of the instructional material, in the manner of transmitting it to the students, in the approach to the students, in the demands which teachers make on the students, in the outer appearance of the students, and especially in their conduct not only outside the school but even during the hours of teaching. Abusive freedom of school youth, we can by no means designate as democratic freedom. Only a person can call it democratic who has no true concept of true democratic order and does not understand the very term democracy as it is clearly defined in Webster's Dictionary.

### Psychological Judgments on Experience

Psychology shows that the satisfaction a person derives from success in one direction leads him to do something else, and this is the chief reason why people of moderate ability, delighted by the fine results of their work, achieve unexpected accomplishments. Their intellectual life also casts a gleam of light on their emotional and moral life. Ethical interests and inclinations revolve around the axis of moral life and the receptibility of the mind. On his moral life depend in large part all the mental efforts of a person. In other words, all branches of experience so intertwine that in disentangling one branch it *willy-nilly* leaves a mark, an impression on another branch which is at the same time the proof of its former existence. This mutual relationship of all branches of experience must always be taken into account in planning programs of instruction and education and all those branches of experience should be developed practically, by proper instruction, and by education in the schools.

The nature of the progress of experience is always dependent upon the efforts of the teacher, beginning with his first word which he speaks to the young people not only in the school during instruction but also outside of its walls. All aspects of experience, as thinking, feeling, desiring, are dependent upon their application by the teacher in the process of instruction. But equilibrium must be achieved between these aspects; therefore, a person must, at the same time, develop physically, intellectually, esthetically, and socially, for actions in one field must be, at least, sufficient to achieve equilibrium with other phases.

All these phases occur in the process of instruction and education. One can observe their source in the program of instruction and education, and teachers must not undervalue any of the educational phases, but must always consider them all in preparing an hour of instruction. So, if our experience is of an educational character, it must at all costs include all these four principles:

1. Exact observation,
2. Clear understanding,
3. Independent thinking,
4. The striving for continuous achievements.

Observing the process of education and instruction, there can be noted the presence of all these four phases, but at once joined as inseparable parts of a whole. For this reason the process of instruction and education must be large in scope to be able to include the actions of all aspects of experience.

The reformers of modern education urge the equal development of all the powers of a person. This argument, then, also strongly pleads for a change in the program of instruction and education in the schools as the first step. A new program must take into account the entire individuality and not only the inclinations of a person that are now needed by the state or industry, such as mathematics and physics. The cultural world, the world of noble productivity, cannot find pleasure in the progress of modern military technique, for everyone sees that this progress is accompanied by the complete isolation and full disregard of the life of a person, taking this primarily in the spiritual sense of the word. This narrow specialization is profitable only for the development of industry and its mass production. It compresses the outlook of a person, his spiritual culture, his views on various problems of life, and makes of him an automaton capable of carrying on strikes and sabotage, including robbery and murder, for such a person has no views of his own, he only performs the will of others which very often is the will of street gangsters and enemies of the state.

Although everybody delights in and is enraptured by the results of narrow specialization, for its brilliant result in industry, yet, we must make every effort that the workman in addition to his narrow occupation also may have a broad view on other problems of life which, perhaps, have little connection with production, for only then will he be materially and morally profitable for the state.

## AUTOMATION

Today, at every step, there can be observed tremendous enthusiasm for automation. Large companies spend huge sums of money on literature, radio, television, advertising, and explanatory films in order to convince their shareholders and the public that automation was created by men expressly for the purpose of making people happy. Certainly, each of us agrees that: Automation represents a new level in the continuing industrial revolution. Because of the power of automation to formalize and to expedite scientific thought production, the consequences of this new technique will have a more profound effect on our civilization than the mere development of other new techniques of manufacture.

In effect, automation is promoting a technological revolution which dwarfs, in significance, the concurrent industrial revolution.[1]

The most common reasons for applying automation are to increase production, reduce costs, make jobs easier and perform jobs that could not otherwise be done.[2]

Automation tends to increase the tempo of everything it touches, and in so doing spreads steadily into new areas . . . Thus automation systems tend to become larger, faster and more complex.[3]

In atomic power plants, automation and remote control are used to avoid the dangers of radiation.

In offices, high-speed electronic computers do accounting and other business operations.[4]

Each of us surely is delighted by the foregoing, but in reading further, the content urges us to more profound consideration:

1. The Encyclopedia Americana, c. 1961.
2. Encyclopaedia Britannica, c. 1962.
3. *Ibid.*
4. *Ibid.*

Automation devices may have the features of being self-powered, self-guiding and self-correcting. They replace and extend human efforts and senses.[1]

The difference between automation and mass production lies in the complete integration of fully automatic machines without the need for man as an intermediary.[2]

Still further, we read:

Automation means the ultimate divorcement of man from the machine as an integral part of its operation.[3]

One can easily compare automation with fire. Fire is most beneficial to a person and even affords him pleasure to some extent, but, at the same time, fire can cause huge material losses, and even death if one uses it under improper circumstances.

Because the development of automation promises to be swift, there is a danger that we shall not be adequately prepared to make the sociological changes necessary to adjust to this new influence in our lives.

To prepare for automation it is first necessary to predict the nature of its probable influence on our lives. This task is especially complicated because automation is not itself clearly understood by even the specialists. Experience in the development of machines and mass production does not exactly parallel the circumstances imposed by automation.[4]

The following conclusion can be made from the foregoing: Automation should be allowed to attain only some sort of secondary status in a state if the state has a tremendous need for it and, at the same time, if the state is short-handed in its labor force. If there must be a production race with other states, a proportional or even accelerated pace should be maintained by various means such as using mechanization, and utilizing automation to some extent if an urgent need arises. If it is not completely necessary, an employee should not be discharged and replaced by an automation. The state of present-day automation

1. *Ibid.*
2. The Encyclopedia Americana, c. 1961.
3. *Ibid.*
4. *Ibid.*

can be likened to a car which loses a wheel in speeding down a highway, and, although the driver desperately tries to control the car, it nevertheless, eventually leaves its intended course.

Automation usually captures the enthusiasm of individuals who plan for immediate objectives. They are the people who wish to profit from automation-products and often are indifferent as to whether the invention will benefit their children and grandchildren.

When pondering on all misfortunes, one comes to the conclusion that high among the greatest of these is unemployment. In other words, this can be called an immoral epidemic, which in a very short period of time breeds immorality among great masses of people. Unemployment cannot be withstood even by those individuals who have been brought up in the most moral spirit and under the best circumstances for such upbringing. A direct question can now be asked: What is the reason for this? There is only one answer to this question. Every person was created to work, for the very physical and psychological nature of every person instinctively demands this. This can best be exemplified by little children who, as soon as they gain a little understanding, want to participate in everything.

Work is even more deeply rooted in the nature of an adult, for the moment that an adult is without work he begins to become ill, and he becomes ill both physically and psychically although quite often he is unaware of this.

Everyone observes how prolonged holidays can affect a person quite adversely. At the end of prolonged holidays, if they have been spent in idleness, the person very often is demoralized to some extent, nothing satisfies him, he views everything indifferently, he complains about everything, and criticizes everybody.

The state must abolish unemployment, because unemployment is like an unnoticeable worm which even attacks hardwood, and it becomes no longer healthy and profitable.

Even if it were possible to perfect automation to the point where it would bring tremendous profits to companies and they could afford to offer permanent paid holidays to their employees, such an inactive life of citizens necessarily would not make a paradise on earth, instead, it possibly could cause a hell on earth.

A person who is capable of working must, of necessity, work constantly. Money should not be doled out to people because of unemployment, but the economy should be so arranged that a citizen should have steady employment. Such employment creates a healthy atmosphere in which, without great difficulties, it is possible for steadily employed fathers to bring up the children into becoming worthwhile citizens.

The question of automation should be considered not only in terms of sociology and economics, but a no lesser voice should also be taken in the matter by the philosophy of instruction and education.

Already, as a result of only partial automation of factories, many fathers walk the streets for months without work and have not the slightest hope of obtaining a job, because automation is getting rid of more-and-more able workers.

In order to understand this misfortune, it is necessary to approach it more closely, which can be done quite easily. Visit the home of an unemployed person. Will it be pleasant to sit there even for five minutes? Will there be something to discuss? Gaze at their disillusioned faces, listen to their constant complaints. What counsel can the church, the school, and the educational organizations give in this case? What theoretical arguments can be used in order to bring up children to be worthwhile citizens when the argument of the actuality in which they live strongly antagonizes them against the state leadership and there are no means, whereby their opinions and lives can be changed?

When we read or hear of the overqualification of the labor force, why was not this worker overqualified when he was still employed in his old place of business, and why was he not transferred to another job after his overqualification?

The matter now stands that even young workers are being released from their jobs. Is society planning to overqualify all workers, or only the very young ones?

The question now arises: What must a person do who is completely able and willing to work but is over thirty-five years of age and has lost his job either due to automation or because his place was taken by a much younger person because the younger person is more profitable to the company, for the company can spend less money on his pension fund and his hospitalization? This is a serious problem, and the state will undoubtedly carefully consider this matter.

In concluding this work with these lines, this writer trusts that he did not write even one word which would cause harm to anybody. In reflecting on the most important tendencies of the development of this book, this author placed observations and analyses of a truly good person as the main subject of his concept. These did not pertain only to his name or to his appearance but to a person as the best exponent of an intelligent creature, for only such a person will be able to solve in a humane fashion all his even most drastic affairs as well as untie the strongest knots of contemporary politics. Therefore, this author is deeply convinced that not even one person will appear who, after having read this book, will have the temerity to throw a stone into the garden where everything which he is cultivating can benefit every person, for every person has the right to profit from its fruits.

# BIBLIOGRAPHY

Adler, Alfred, *Education of the Individual*, New York, Philosophical Lib., 1958.

Aitken, William Ewart Maurice, *Teaching a Child*, Toronto, W. J. Gage & So., 1957.

Alexander, William Marvin, and Saylor, J. G., *Modern Secondary Education;* Basic Principles and Practices, New York, Rinehart, 1959.

Alexander, William Marvin, and Halverson, P.M., *Effective Teaching in Secondary Schools*, New York, Rinehart, 1956.

Allen, Mary Louise, *Education or Indoctrination*, Caldwell, Caxton Printers, 1955.

Anderson, Edna A., *Round the Clock in the Classroom*, Minneapolis, Dennison & Co., 1959.

Andrews, Michael F., (Ed.) *Aesthetic Form and Education*, Syracuse, Syracuse Univ. Press, 1958.

Baker, Melvin C., *Foundations of John Dewey's Educational Theory*, New York, Columbia Univ. Press, 1955.

Barnes, John B., *Educational Research for Classroom Teachers*, New York, Putnam, 1960.

Bass, Bernard M., *Leadership, Psychology, and Organizational Behavior*, New York, Harper, 1960.

Bayles, Ernest Edward, *Democratic Educational Theory*, New York, Harper, 1960.

Bent, Rudyard Kipling and Kronenberg, *Principles of Secondary Education*, Toronto, McGraw-Hill, 1955.

Benz, Stanley Carroll, *Investigation of the Attributes and Techniques of High School Counselors*, Lafayette, Ind., Purdue Univ., 1958.

Bereday, George Zygmunt Fijalkowski, and Volpicelli, Luigi (Eds.), *Public Education in America*, New York, Harper, 1958.

Bettelheim, Bruno, *Truants from Life; Rehabilitation of Emo-
tionally Disturbed Children*, Glencoe, Free Press, 1955.

Bhatia, Hansraj, *New Deal in Secondary Education*, New York,
Longmans, 1959.

Bingham, Alma Irene, *Improving Children's Facility in Problem
Solving*, New York, Teachers Col., 1958.

Bisno, Herbert, *Place of the Undergraduate Curriculum in Social
Work Education*, New York, Council on Social Work, Ed., 1959.

Bloom, Benjamin S. and others, *Are the Schools Meeting the
Child's Needs?*, Chicago, Univ. of Chicago Press, 1952.

Boehm, Werner William, *Objectives of the Social Work Curriculum of the Future*, New York, Council on Social Work, Ed.,
1959.

Bonney, Merl Edwin, *Mental Health in Education*, Englewood
Cliffs, Allyn & Bacon, 1960.

Bossard, James Herbert Siward, *Sociology of Child Development*,
New York, Harper, 1954.

Bossing, Nelson Louis, *Principles of Secondary Education;* and
other essays and addresses; Ed. by R. M. Gay, Boston, 1955.

Bruner, Jerome Seymour, *Process of Education*, Cambridge, Harvard Univ. Press., 1960.

Bucher, Charles Augustus, and Reade, E. M., *Physical Education
in the Modern Elementary School*, New York, Macmillan, 1958.

Bühler, Karl, *Mental Development of the Child*, New York, Hu-
manities Press, 1954.

Burkard, William Edwin and others, *Health and Human Welfare*,
Chicago, Lyons & Carnahan, 1956.

Burton, Dwight L., *Literature Study in the High Schools*, Chicago,
Holt, 1959.

Burton, William Henry, *Guidance of Learning Activities;* a summary of the principles of learning based upon the growth of the
learner, New York, Appleton, 1952.

Byram, Harold Moore, and Wenrich, R. C., *Vocational Education
and Practical Arts in the Community School*, New York, Macmillan, 1956.

Carron, Mancolm, and Cavanaugh, A. D. (Eds.) *Readings in
The Philosophy of Education*, Detroit, Univ. of Detroit, 1959.

Cassel, Russell Napoleon, *Psychology of Child Discipline*, Cincin-
nati, C. A. Gregory Co., 1955.

Child Study Association of America, *Facts of Life for Children;*
Ed. by A. Suehsdorf, Indianapolis, Bobbs-Merrill Co., 1954.

Coladarci, Arthur Paul (Ed.) *Educational Psychology;* Book of
Readings. Dryden, 1955.

Cole, Luella Winifred, *Psychology of Adolescence,* New York,
Rinehart, 1959.

Conant, Howard Somers, and Randall, A. W., *Art in Education,*
Peoria, Bennett, 1959.

Cook, Kermit A. and others, *Student Teaching in the Secondary
School,* Dubuque, Brown, 1954.

Crow, Alice (Von Bauer) (Mrs. Lester Donald Crow), *Outline
of Educational Psychology,* Littlefield, Adams & Co., 1956.

Crow, Lester Donald, and Crow, A. V., *Adolescent Development
and Adjustment,* Toronto, McGraw-Hill, 1956.

Crow, Lester Donald, and Crow, A. V., *Introduction to Education,* New Rev. Ed., New York, Am. Bk., 1960.

Crow, Lester Donald, and Crow, A. V., *Introduction to Education: Fundamental Principles and Modern Practices,* Rev. Ed.,
New York, Am. Bk., 1954.

Cruze, Wendell Wayne, *Adolescent Psychology and Development,*
New York, Ronald, 1953.

Curtis, Stanley James, *Introduction to the Philosophy of Education,* London, Univ. Tutorial Press, 1958.

Cutts, Norma Estelle, and Moseley, Nicholas, *Teaching the Bright
and Gifted,* Englewood Cliffs, Prentice-Hall, 1957.

DeMaria, Robert, *Theme Correction Guide,* New York, Holt,
1957.

D'Evelyn, Katherine E., *Meeting Children's Emotional Needs;* A
guide for teachers, Englewood Cliffs, Prentice-Hall, 1957.

Devereux, George, *Therapeutic Education; its Theoretical Bases
and Practice,* New York, Harper, 1956.

Dewey, John, *Moral Principles in Education,* Boston, Houghton
Mifflin Co., 1909.

Dressel, Paul Leroy (Ed.), *Evaluation in General Education,*
Dubuque, Brown, 1954.

Dressel and Mayhew, L. B., *Critical Thinking in Social Science,*
Dubuque, Brown, 1954.

Driscoll, Gertrude Porter, *Child Guidance in the Classroom,* New
York Teachers Col., 1955.

Dubay Thomas, *Philosophy of the State as Educator*, Milwaukee, Bruce Pub., 1959.

Eng, Helga Kristine, *Psychology of Child and Youth Drawing from the Ninth to the Twenty-Fourth Year*, London, Routledge, 1957.

Finney, Ross Lee, *A Sociological Philosophy of Education*, New York, MacMillan, 1928.

Fischer, E. Harian, *Teaching Can Be Fun!*, New York, William-Frederick Press, 1957.

Fleck, Henrietta Christina, and others, *Exploring Home and Family Living*, Englewood Cliffs, Prentice-Hall, 1959.

Fleming, Charlotte Mary, *Social Psychology of Education*, London, Routledge, 1960.

Frandsen, Arden N., *How Children Learn; An educational Psychology*, Toronto, McGraw-Hill, 1957.

Frank, Lawrence Kelso, *School as Agent for Cultural Renewal*, Cambridge, Harvard Univ. Press, 1959.

Fraser, Ellen D. and others, *Child and Physical Education*, Englewood Cliffs, Prentice-Hall, 1956.

Froebel, Friedrich, *Education of Man*, New York, Appleton, 1887.

Giles, Hermann H., *Human Dynamics and Human Relations Education*, New York, N. Y. Univ. Press, 1954.

Giles, Hermann H., *Education and Human Motivation*, New York, Philosophical Lib., 1957.

Gottsegen, Monroe George, and Gottsegen, G. B. (Eds.), *Professional School Psychology*, New York, Grune & Stratton, Inc., 1960.

Gould, Sir Ronald, and Carr, W. G., *How to Improve the Caliber of Teaching*, Washington, D.C., Merkle Press, 1959.

Greenlee, Julian Marion, *Teaching Science to Children*, Dubuque, Brown, 1955.

Guerard, Albert Leon, *Education of a Humanist*, Cambridge, Harvard Univ. Press, 1949.

Gwynn, John Minor, *Curriculum Principles and Social Trends*, 3rd Ed., New York, MacMillan, 1960.

Hahn, Milton Edwin, and MacLean, M. S., *Counseling Psychology*, 2nd Ed., Toronto, McGraw-Hill, 1955.

Hansen, Kenneth Harvey, *Philosophy for American Education*, Englewood Cliffs, Prentice-Hall, 1960.

Haskew, Laurence De Fee, *Discipline of Education and America's Future*, Pittsburgh, Univ. of Pittsburgh Press, 1959.

Henry, V. Horatio, *New Social Studies Methodology*, Jackson, Miss., Jackson State Col., 1958.

Herbart, Johann F., *Allgemeine Pädagogik und Umriss pädagogischer Vorlesungen*, Leipzig, Siegismund & Volkening, 1876.

Hood, Fred Carlisle, *Developing the Ability to Assess the Results of Thinking*, Urbana, Ill., Univ. of Ill., 1949.

Horne, Herman Harrell, *The Philosophy of Education*, New York, MacMillan, 1930.

Hughes, Arthur George, and Hughes, E. H., *Education*, Some Fundamental Problems, A discussion book for students of education, New York, Longmans, 1960.

Hymes, James Lee, Jr., *Behavior and Misbehavior; Teachers Guide to Action*, Englewood Cliffs, Prentice-Hall, 1955.

Irwing, Leslie William, and others, *Methods and Materials in School Health Education*, St. Louis, Mosby, 1956.

Jacobsen, Henry, *How to Teach Adults*, Wheaton, Ill., Scripture Press, 1957.

Johnston, Edgar Grant, and others, *Role of the Teacher in Guidance*, Englewood Cliffs, Prentice-Hall, 1959.

Jones, Richard M., *Application of Psychoanalysis to Education*, Springfield, Thomas, 1960.

Judges, Arthur Valentine (Ed.), *Function of Teaching;* Seven approaches to purpose, tradition and environment, Toronto, British Bk. Service Ltd., 1959.

Kant, Immanuel, *Education*, Ann Arbor, Univ. of Mich. Press, 1960.

Kerrison, Irvine, L. H. and Levine, H. A., *Labor Leadership Education*, A union university approach, New Brunswick, Rutgers Univ. Press, 1960.

Kerschensteiner, Georg M. A., *Die Pädagogik der Gegenwart in Selbstdarstellungen*, herausgegeben von E. Hahn, Bd. I, Leipzig, 1926.

Lawson, Reed, *Learning and Behavior*, New York, MacMillan, 1960.

Lieberman, Myron, *Future of Public Education*, Chicago, Univ. of Chicago Press, 1960.

Lindquist, Everett Franklin, *Design and Analysis of Experiments in Psychology and Education*, Boston, Houghton, 1953.

Loughary, John W., *Counseling in Secondary Schools*, New York, Harper, 1961.

Lurie, Harry Lawrence, *Community Organization Method in Social Work Education*, New York, Council on Social Work, Ed., 1959.

Mann, Horace, *Republic and the School*, New York, Teachers Col., 1957.

Maritain, Jacques, *Education at the Crossroads*, New Haven, Yale Univ. Press, 1960.

Mason, Robert Emmett, *Educational Ideals in American Society*, Englewood Cliffs, Allyn & Bacon, 1960.

Mathewson, Robert Hendry, *Guidance Policy and Practice*, New York, Harper, 1949.

Mayer, Frederick, *Education for Creative Living*, New York, Whittier, 1959.

Mayer, Frederick, *Goals of Education*, New York, Public Affairs Press, 1960.

Mayhew, Lewis B. (Ed.), *General Education*, New York, Harper, 1960.

McDonald, Milo Francis, *American Education:* Old, the Modern and the New, New York, Am. Ed. Assn., 1952.

McKinney, Fred, *Psychology of Personal Adjustment;* Students' instruction to mental hygiene, New York, Wiley, 1960.

Mencher, Samuel, *Research Method in Social Work Education*, New York, Council on Social Work, Ed., 1959.

Merrill, Mrs. Helen Lawrence, *Science Teacher in Action*, Boston, Christopher, 1956.

Michaelis, John U., *Social Studies For Children in a Democracy,* Englewood Cliffs, Prentice-Hall, 1956.

deMontaigne, Michael E., *Essais,* Paris, Librairie Garnier frères, Vol. III. 1948.

Morris, Charles Eugene, *Counseling with Young People,* New York, Assn. Press, 1954.

Mortensen, Donald G. and Schmuller, A.M., *Guidance in Today's Schools,* New York, Wiley, 1959.

Nelson, Leslie Weldemar, and McDonald, Blanche, *Guide to Student Teaching,* Rev. Ed., Dubuque, Brown, W.C., 1958.

Newman, Harry and Sidney, D.M., *Teaching Management;* A practical handbook with special reference to the case study method, London, Rutledge, 1955.

Niblett, William Roy, *Education and the Modern Mind,* London, Faber, 1954.

Niblett, William Roy, *Education: The Lost Dimension,* New York, W. Sloane Associates, 1955.

Oliver, Robert A., *Effective Teaching,* Don Mills, Dent & Sons Ltd., 1956.

Oliver, Robert A., *Effective Teaching;* A guide to general methods, Rev. Ed., Canadian Teachers' Professional Lib., 1960.

O'Neill, Reginald F., *Theories of Knowledge,* Englewood Cliffs, Prentice-Hall, 1960.

Ottaway, Andrew Kenneth Cosway, *Education and Society;* Introduction to the Sociology of Education, London, Routledge, 1953.

Pearson, Ralph M., *New Art Education,* Rev. Ed., New York, Harper, 1953.

Peters, Richard Stanley, *Authority, Responsibility and Education,* New York, Taplinger, 1960.

Pintner, Rudolf and others, *Educational Psychology,* New York, Barnes & Noble, 1956.

Preston, Ralph Clausius, *Teaching Study Habits and Skills,* New York, Rinehart, 1959.

Pumphrey, Mrs. Muriel (Warren), *Teaching of Values and Ethics in Social Work Education,* New York, Council on Social Work, Ed., 1959.

Rasey, Marie I., *Toward Maturity: The Psychology of Child Development*, New York, Barnes & Noble, 1957.

Rathbone, Josephine Langworthy, *Corrective Physical Education*, Philadelphia, Saunders, 1959.

Rebentisch, Alice, *How to Help Your Child with Schoolwork*, Miami, Universal Books, 1955.

Redl, Fritz and Wattenberg, W. W., *Mental Hygiene in Teaching*, Chicago, Harcourt, 1959.

Remmers, Hermann Henry, and others, *Study Manual for Introduction to Educational Psychology*, New York, Harper, 1954.

Rogers, William C., *Community Education in World Affairs*, Minneapolis, Univ. of Minn., 1956.

Roucek, Joseph Slabey, *Challenge of Science Education*, New York, Philosophical Lib., 1959.

Rusk, Robert Robertson, *Doctrines of the Great Educators*, New York, St. Martin's Press, 1954.

Russell, David Harris, *Children Thinking*, Toronto, Ginn, 1956.

Sargent, William Ernest, *Teach Yourself Psychology*, New York, Roy Pubs., 1955.

Schwartz, Milton M. and Kerrison, I.L.H., *Learning Process, with Applications to Workers' Education*, New Brunswick, Rutgers Univ. Inst., 1956.

Seagoe, May V., *Teacher's Guide to the Learning Process*, Dubuque, Brown, W. C., 1956.

Sechrest, Carolyn A., *New Dimensions in Counseling Students*, New York Teachers Col., 1958.

Shuster, George Nauman, *Education and Moral Wisdom*, New York, Harper, 1960.

*Shlyakh Navchannya ta Vykhovannya* (Journal) Lviv, October-November-December, 1933.

Skinner, Charles Edward, (Ed.), *Educational Psychology*, 4th Ed., Englewood Cliffs, Prentice-Hall, 1959.

Smith, Glenn Erie, *Counseling in the Secondary School*, New York, MacMillan, 1955.

Snow, Robert H., *Community Adult Education;* Methods of organizing and maintaining learning opportunities for men and women, New York, Putnam, 1955.

Stack, Herbert James and others (Eds.), *Education for Safe Living*, Englewood Cliffs, Prentice-Hall, 1949.

Staton, Thomas Felix, *How to Instruct Successfully;* modern teaching methods in adult education, Toronto, McGraw-Hill, 1960.
Still, Joseph William, *Science and Education at the Crossroads,* Washington, D.C., Public Affairs Press, 1958.
Studt, Elliot, *Education for Social Workers in the Correctional Study,* New York, Council on Social Work Ed., 1959.
Sweeney, Stephen B. and Davy, T. J. (Eds.), *Education for Administrative Careers in Government Service,* Philadelphia, Univ. of Pa. Press, 1958.

Tabor, Francis H., *Rocks of True Teaching,* New York, E. C. Berkeley Associates, 1959.
Tead, Ordway, *Character Building and Higher Education* (Kappa Delta Pi Lecture Ser.), New York, Macmillan, 1953.
Teicher, Joseph David, *Your Child and His Problems;* A basic guide for parents, Boston, Little, 1953.
Thompson, George Greene and others, *Educational Psychology;* Student workbook, New York, Appleton, 1959.
Thorpe, Louis Peter, *Child Psychology and Development,* 2nd Ed., New York, Ronald, 1955.

Valentine, Charles Wilfrid, *Parents and Children;* First book on the psychology of child development and training, New York, Philosophical Lib., 1955.
Van Dalen, Deobold B. and Brittell, R. W., *Looking Ahead to Teaching,* Englewood Cliffs, Allyn & Bacon, 1959.
Vashchenko, Hryhoriy, *Tilovykhovannya yak Zasib Vykhovannya Voli i Kharakteru,* Munich, Druckgenossenschaft "Cicero" G.m.b.H., 1956.
Vashchenko, Hryhoriy, *Osnovy Estetychnoho Vykhovannya,* Munich, "Avangard" publisher, 1957.
Vashchenko, Hryhoriy, *Vykhovannya Voli i Kharakteru,* London, Caplin and Co., Press Ltd. Croy don, 1952, P. I.
Vashchenko, Hryhoriy, *Vykhovannya Voli i Kharakteru,* Munich, Druckgenossenschaft "Cicero" G.m.b.H., 1959, P. II.

Walsh, Ann Marie, *Self-Concepts of Bright Boys with Learning Difficulties,* New York, Teachers Co., 1956.
Weed, P. C., Jr., *Religion the Essence of Education,* New York, Morehouse-Gorham Co., 1955.

Wellington, Charles Burleigh and Wellington, J. W., *Teaching for Critical Thinking*, with emphasis on secondary education, Toronto, McGraw-Hill, 1960.

Weiss, Thomas Michael, and Hoover, K. H., *Scientific Foundations of Education*, Dubuque, Brown, W. C., 1960.

Weissman, Irving, *Social Welfare Policy and Services in Social Work Education*, New York, Council on Social Work, Ed., 1959.

Wheat, Harry Grove, *Foundations of School Learning*, New York, Alfred A. Knopf, 1955.

Whitehead, Alfred North, *Aims of Education and other Essays*, London, E. Benn, Ltd., 1955.

Wiles, Kimball, *Teaching for Better Schools*, 2nd Ed., Englewood Cliffs, Prentice-Hall, 1959.

Wiles, Kimball, *Supervision for Better Schools;* Role of the official leader in program development, Englewood Cliffs, Prentice-Hall, 1955.

Wiles, Kimball, *Teaching for Better Schools*, Englewood Cliffs, Prentice-Hall, 1952.

Weber, Karl J., *Ästhetic als pädagogische Grundwissenschaft*, Berlin, Wiegandt und Grieben, 1852.

Yoakam, Gerald Alan, *Basic Reading Instruction*, Toronto, McGraw-Hill, 1955.

Zirbes, Laura, *Spurs to Creative Teaching*, New York, Putnam, 1959.

Zubek, John Peter, and Solberg, P. A., *Human Development*, Toronto, McGraw-Hill, 1954.

*Encyclopedias*

1. The Encyclopedia Americana, c. 1961.
2. Encyclopaedia Britannica, c. 1962.

# INDEX

## A

Absolute Idea, 90
Acceptance, passive, of knowledge, 70
Achievements, scholastic, 85
Acquaintance of the pupil with life: To understand life, 20; How to approach it?, 20
Activity of the teacher, 4
Age, atomic, 64
Aims of developing dominating interests, 19
American high schools, 71
Amusements as a means of intellectual development, 130
Aristotle, 154
Art of education, 4
Aspects of education, 4
Atlantic Ocean, VII
Atmosphere, suitable, XIX
Attention, chief, 68
Automation, VIII, 170-173
Authority of teacher-educator, 29
Awareness of purpose, 146

## B

Bacon, 105
Basis, chief, for training patriotism, 84
Benefits, practical, IX

## C

Calling as such, 29
Calling of a teacher, 38

Caplin and Co., 61
Categories of: people, 30; soul, 65
Causes, fundamental, 4
Cause of the loss of character; What is the cause of moral decline?, 49
Causes which influence the health of child positively and negatively, 131
Cell, primitive, 65
Characteristic, peculiar, of the adolescent, 62
Characteristics: physical, XVIII psychical, XVIII;
Characteristics of an ideally educated person, 23-24
Characterization of temperaments, 89
Christ, 44
Christianity, 126
Cicero, 133
Classification of work, 67
Concept of universal education, 149
Conditions, physical, XIX
Consciousness of citizenship, XX
Conversations, numerous, VIII
Cooperation, knowledgeable, of the teacher, 42
Course of education, 25-28
Creativity, independent, 69
Creator, XIX
Croydon, 61

## D

Darwin, 58

Definitions of: Attention, 55; Char-
    acter, 22; Culture, 21; Demo-
    cracy, 124; Discipline, 22; Know-
    ledge, 22; Productivity, 22; "To
    Educate", 27, 42
Demonstration, chief division of
    education, 23
Development of: child, XVIII;
    criteria of reason, 61; human-
    ity, 9; individuals, 114; society,
    113
Development: esthetic, 97; inde-
    pendent, XVIII; present, social,
    43
Devices, methodological, 70
Dewey, John, XVII, 5, 28, 37
Dignity of student, 107
Discipline: external, 81; internal, 81
Disciplines of instruction, XVIII

                    E

Education: civic, 113; ethical, 103;
    esthetic, XIX, 97, 100, 101; gen-
    eral, VII; modern, VIII, XVIII,
    48, 105; social, 113
Education, our idea of, VII, XVI,
    42, 52, 83
Education as a conscious progress,
    9
Education, esthetic: First steps in
    esthetic education; the principles
    of esthetic education; the school
    is the basis of esthetic education;
    theoretical and practical studies
    of art, 93-96
Education for health and produc-
    tivity, 129, 133
Education from perspective of the
    present day, 36
Education in two directions: 1. The
    insuring of the development of
    the individual, 2. The individual
    must bring profit to society, 118-
    120

Educator, VII
Energy, psychic, 70
Environment, communal and edu-
    cation, 45, 46. See also: Auto-
    mation, 170-173
Ethics, educational, XIX
Exercise of the will, 64
Experience in hours of instruc-
    tion, 153
Experiments as: aim of education,
    22; such, 150; test, 151
Experiments, biological, 68
Eye, critical, VII

                    F

Factors in the improvement of
    educational work, 145, 146
Facts, individual, 4
Folkesch, J., 100
Foreword, VII
Formation of personality, 82
Freedom, democratic, 123
Freedom of: choice, 106; individ-
    ual, 79
Freud, 108

                    G

Goal of democratic education, 126
Goal of progress of a person, 15
Government bodies, VII
Government in society, 120-122
Growth of the child: spiritual, in-
    tellectual, physical, 5-6
Gymnasium, classical, 71

                    H

Habits, 114
Health of teacher, 41
Hemispheres, eastern and western,
    VIII
Herbart, Johann, 105, 107, 150,
    153, 154
Heritage, social, in education, 44

Hippocrates, 88
Honor, 81
How to live?, 12
Hypothesis of materialists, 64

I

Idea and its importance, 91-93
Ideal of education, XVI, XVII
Ideal of freedom, 163
Ideal, pedagogical, 97
Idealism in education, 90
Idealists, 64, 90
Importance of: labor, 64; environ-
   ment in process of esthetic edu-
   cation, 98. *See also*: Automa-
   tion, 170-173
Instruction, visual, 67
Intelligence, political, 117
Intelligence of a teacher, 31
Introduction, XV-XX
Intuition, 31

J

James, XVII
Judgments, psychological, on experience, 167

K

Kerschensteiner, Georg, 27, 37
Kinds of heritage, 44
Knowledge of: physical nature of
   child, 42; sports, 42
Knowledge, theoretical, 148
Komensky, 154
Kretschmer, 88

L

Law of freedom, 123
Leibnitz, 141
Leshaft, 88
Life of primitive man, 44
Limit, deeper, in teaching, 36
Locke, 154

M

Macrocosm, XIX, 166
Man: modern, XVI; moral, 81
Material: educational, VIII, 27-28;
   extensive, 69; scholarly, 69
Materialism, 90
Materialists, 64
Method-definitions: broader, 137;
   narrow, 137
Method of: application, XX; edu-
   cation, VII, 137; instruction, 7,
   137, 138; life, XVII
Microcosm, XIX, 166
Middle Ages, 69
Mode of thinking, 4
Montaigne de, Michel, 101, 153
Morality, religious, 80
Morals as the basis of education:
   Morals at the present time; the
   revival of morality; the power of
   morality; the sources of morality; moral education; four methods by which morality is transplanted to youth from parents
   and the schools; moral principles; the morality of persons
   cannot be artificial; moral man
   is, first of all, a disciplined man;
   determination, another quality
   of a moral person, 73-82
Morpheus, 154

N

Nature of: child, 52; experience,
   150; instruction, 13-14
Nature of instruction and education in the new school: The idea
   of schooling; the task of the
   school; the quality of education,
   13-14
Nietzsche, 141

O

Object of educational activity, 26, 140
Objective of the new system, 163
Objectivity, 53
Opinion: broader, 7; public, 45
Overworking — its unhealthy results, 66-68

P

Participation in pedagogical process, 43
Patriotism, 83
Pedagogue in our conception, 43
Pedagogy, XIX
Pedantry, 42
Perfection, principal goal, 23
Periods of: infant; adolescence; young adulthood, 60-63
Person: disciplined, 81; of principle, 80, 81; worthy, envisioned, VIII
Pestalozzi, 39, 154
Philosophy as a foundation of education: The term-philosophy; the educational doctrines; the practical application of philosophical views; philosophy as core of all principles and worthy motives, 1, 2. *See also*: The Task of Philosophy, 3
Philosophy as science, XV
Philosophy of: education VII, VIII, XIX, 4; life, 5, 41
Plato, 1, 3, 12, 92, 100
Power of the will in education, 59
Powers, spiritual, XVIII
Preface, VIII
Presentation, classical, VII
Principles of philosophy, XVI
Principles of educational method: The chief task in erecting prin-
ciples; the essence of proper result in instruction and education, 142-145
Problems, educational: The problem of health; of relaxation; economic problem; of family life; the problem of progress; the place of the individual in society, 16
Process, educational, XIX, 4, 7
Process, natural, 47
Process of formation of character, 80
Production of atomic power, XV
Programs, educational, and training, VIII
Programs of instruction, 71
Punishment, corporal, 37, 39, 40
Purpose of education, 16, 17

Q

Questions, philosophical, VIII, IX

R

Reflect of family on society, 46
Reform of educational system, 159
Religion, 80
Responsibility of the pedagogue, 33
Rest: physical; psychic, 66-68
Role of the will, 53
Rousseau, Jean Jacques, 34, 154
Rules of government in democratic states, 45

S

Salvation Army, 161
Sanctions, democratic, 126
Scale of living, 122
Schools, elementary and secondary, VII, VIII, IX
School — old and new, 13
School as: the basis of esthetic education, 97; a source of experience, 164

School in a democratic system of government, 124
Self-development, 68; — education, 68, 72, 106, 109
Shlyakh Navchanya ta Vykhovanya, 70
Sketch, historical, 44
Society, unhealthy, 121
Spencer, 1, 100
Stone Age, 48, 65
Structures, social, 114
Struggle of motives, 62
Studies, theoretical and practical, 99
System: democratic, 124; dominant, XVII; educational, VII, VIII, XVII; modern, VIII, 72; particular, VIII

T

Talents: Who has them? How many does one have? 30
Talents, unused, 57
Task of education, 19, 46, 102, 106
Task, main, of a teacher, 32
Task of: modern education, 134; philosophy, 3
Teacher, modern, 5
Tendencies, natural, as the starting point of: activity, 36; moral, 38

Temperament, 88
Temperature, 68
Term-Education, 11
Theories of "free education," 34
Theory of authoritarian education, 34
Theory of idealists, 64-66
Times, modern, 82
Tolstoy, 43
Tradition as the basis of education, 48

U

University in Ohio, VII
Utilitarianism, 70

V

Values of learning, 13
Vashchenko, Hryhoriy, 35, 61, 62, 84, 96, 112, 133
Vivaciousness, 87

W

Weber, Karl, 100, 101
Webster's Dictionary, 124
Weissman, 45
Work: intellectual, VII; pedagogical, VII; independent, XVIII
Work as the chief means of forming will and character, 63

DATE DUE